The Failure of Marketing

The Failure of Marketing

Why Your Company Isn't
A Growth Machine

Jack Trytten

To order additional copies of this book, contact:
Xlibris Corporation
1-888-795-4274
www.Xlibris.com
Orders@Xlibris.com
44275

CONTENTS

Introduction

Growth

Growth.

Running a growing company is fun. Exciting. Rewarding.

> Hiring is more fun than firing.

> New products are more exciting than "value engineering."

> Investing is more interesting than "pruning."

The CEOs of growing companies are interviewed by *Forbes*, with maybe their picture on the cover. CEOs of companies in trouble get their picture on the cover of *Ridicule* magazine with a tough article inside.

Growth is much more fun, more satisfying. You're going to like it better.

Yes, your company's growing, your industry's growing and the economy's growing. Straight line extrapolation, ever upward.

Life is good.

Now, get real. Here's a little cold water. Isn't there a little bothersome whispering in the back of your mind? A little nagging doubt?

Are you growing faster than your competitors? Are you setting the foundation for future growth? Do you have a realistic growth plan, specific goals, actions, responsibilities?

Or are you just moving with the times, enjoying the ride, thinking this will go on forever?

Are you setting up your company for that cover of *Ridicule?*

In my thirty years of consulting with a wide variety of both consumer goods and B2B firms, I have met more companies who go with the flow, setting themselves up for sales declines in growing markets. Their competitors are preparing to eat their lunch.

Why?

Why do companies that have been wildly successful lose their way?

What is it to lose your way? What's really happening?

When the economy is growing, CEOs look for growth. And when the economy's headed south, the CEO turns away from growth and focuses instead on cutting costs.

How odd. Doesn't this seem backward? Shouldn't you *always* manage your costs? Can't you *grow* in a down economy?

The idea of continual emphasis on growth has not taken hold—except at a few uncommon companies.

The Failure of Marketing

Why give up on managing the top line? Why focus on the cost side of the income statement whenever the economy becomes tight?

Is this because management of the top line (sales) is illusory at best, even during expansions? Does it seem that efforts to grow sales require significant resources (money) that seem to have no direct relationship to results—scarce resources when income is tight?

Why is management of the top line so illusory? As this is being written, the economy is good, some say excellent. But a significant number of companies, large ones, are withdrawing their forecasts, missing their estimates, not because their costs are unexpectedly rising but because they are unable to accurately forecast demand.

Don't companies know what their customers want? Or how much or how many? And how are you to manage what you can't control? How do you manage what you don't know?

Perhaps there's no answer.

Yet, a few uncommon companies do this very well. They know with uncanny accuracy.

It's not that they have continual growth. But during contractions, they contract less than their competitors; during expansions, they expand more.

What do they know that you don't know?

Marketing.

But, perhaps not the marketing you practice.

That's what this book is about.

The kind of marketing that results in growth faster than your competitors, year after year, good times and bad.

Companies that understand this kind of marketing—different from most of the marketing practiced today—are rare.

The rest of the companies are, well, to some degree, marketing failures. Many, deep down, view marketing as a pain. A very expensive pain.

But these companies are in "good" company. It's a big crowd.

Because great marketing *is* different.

It requires different talents and skills. Different management styles. Different measurements.

But most important, great marketing requires a different attitude. Not just on the part of the CMO but all through the company.

And if your managers don't have the right attitude, can't get the right tools, if your systems fail to generate the right measurements, you're going to suffer (if you haven't already) a continual flow of marketing failures.

Expensive, frustrating, failures.

This doesn't have to be. Early on, my first mentor gave me two tips that are worth more than an MBA:

- If you aren't getting the right answer, you're not asking the right question
- Working smarter beats working harder

Marketing Failures

This book is about asking the right questions. Getting the right answers. And, working smarter to get more productive marketing.

The Failure of Marketing

This book is about marketing failures. The most common, the most serious and the most expensive.

While there are always new ways to screw up almost anything, by the end of this book, you'll be exposed to the critical failures of marketing.

Failures of marketing strategy.

Failures of marketing tactics.

Why? Because that's how we learn.

Some of the time.

Unfortunately, the learning is often by trial and error—expensive failures.

There are companies that err, again and again. Over and over. It's not that they're not trying to learn, they just can't figure it out.

Very expensive.

By discussing the failures here, it costs you only the price of the book. And you get to learn while someone else does the failing.

Not a bad deal. You will learn how to focus your marketing on continual growth. Oh, sure, you're still going to stumble but you're going to have a different, more productive framework for learning from those failures.

And you'll most likely avoid the big ones. The ones that have *Ridicule* calling for your picture.

Finally, just think on this:

> How would your business be different if you could:
>
> Have a steady base of loyal—loyal—customers?
>
> Accurately predict future sales?

Have your customers tell you what new products they'd like?

Have a resulting steady stream of successful new products?

Have control over your distribution channels?

Have the highest margins in your industry?

Your life would be different. And much more fun. Don't you suppose?

Let's start with a little history—where did marketing come from?

Part 1: In the beginning . . . .

One might think that modern marketing theory would have come about in a period of great need to grow the top line.

Hardly. In fact, the first exponent of the theory brought it forth early in a period of unbridled growth for our economy. When companies were selling everything they could make.

Necessity was not the mother of this invention.

Actually, modern marketing theory came as an offshoot of general management theory which was the needed necessity at that time.

It's a great story. Take some time to savor it. We haven't had an economy like this since.

And it sets a great stage for failures.

Chapter 1

The Genesis of Marketing

Modern marketing came about during the convergence of remarkable factors, none of which alone would have led to its creation:

The fastest period of growth in American business history

The incredible growth of new technologies

Phenomenal growth in personal income

The coming of age of national distribution

The introduction of the most powerful form of advertising

A dramatic increase in the complexity of business

The new need for management of large numbers of people across great distances

This was truly a remarkable time. And hidden within it was the development of modern marketing.

"May You Live In Fascinating Times" (*Chinese curse*)

Wow, the 1950s. What a time to be alive. On one hand the decade started with the Korean War, price and commodity controls, the threat of Communism, the McCarthy hearings, and progressed to bomb shelters, Sputnik and the beat generation.

But on the other side of the ledger was the roaring economy, the new medium, television, prosperity, jobs, the end of polio, the dramatic growth of the suburbs, and, of course, rock and roll. Most of all, the future looked bright after a decade of depression followed by close to a decade of war.

That war, however, was the genesis of major changes in our economy, in business and how we conduct it. Coming out of the war, The US enjoyed the only strong economic engine of the world. And did it work. Demand had been held back through the serial effects of the depression, WWII and the Korean War. America now supplied the world as the ravaged countries rebuilt their economies.

The intense focus on research and development for the war effort had produced an abundance of new technologies, ready for application to peacetime uses, particularly in materials and electronics.

"I have one word for you, Benjamin. Plastics."

(Mr. Robinson's advice to Benjamin, "The Graduate")

While uttered some 17 years later, this summed up much of the technical progress from the war efforts. Nylon, invented by

DuPont in 1935 and which many males think of as the ultimate plastic, saw the first major consumer market replacing silk in ladies' stockings spurred by the need for silk during the war. By the end of the '50s it was everywhere: toothbrushes, fishing line, automobile and appliance parts, and, of course, wall-to-wall carpet, the signature product of suburbia. And it was only one of many plastics, including the ever-popular polyester.

While DuPont recognized how ubiquitous plastics could become, not even IBM saw that each of us would have a computer sitting on our desks at work with another one—or two—at home. But the computer, aided by the invention of the transistor in 1948 by Shockley at Bell Labs, saw life in the '50s as IBM began its domination of what would revolutionize all phases of business.

But the most obvious change was the mushrooming of suburbia.

"Little boxes on the hillside, little boxes made of ticky tacky, little boxes, little boxes, little boxes all the same,"

("Little Boxes" words and music by Malvina Reynolds)

Malvina, 63 when she wrote that song, sure didn't see the world the way many did during the fifties. To have lived through the 20% unemployment and soup kitchens of the thirties, survived WWII and the Korean War, and now to have your own single family house on your own lot, well this was just too much to dream.

Maybe they did all look alike; maybe they were just ticky tacky, but to those who owned them, who had suffered, who had fought, they were theirs. And this was the fifties.

Growth like never before—or after

During the early decades of the 1900s, the economy grew about 30% every ten years. The decade of the depression was about a third of this normal growth while the 1940s had an astounding growth rate of 72%. This was due to the war production as the GDP declined in both 1946 and 1949. But rapid growth picked up during the fifties as the economy took off, initially fueled by the Korean War and followed by increasing domestic and international demand.

Decade	Growth
1900-09	31.5%
1910-19	31.5
1920-29	40.7
1930-39	10.0
1940-49	72.0
1950-59	49.4
1960-69	54.2
1970-79	37.4
1980-89	35.0
1990-99	35.6

The growth in domestic GDP was almost 50% for the decade of the 1950s and this growth continued right through the sixties.

International demand was important to this growth. Prior to the depression, the US accounted for approximately 20% of the world's GDP with about 6% of the world's population. In 1950, the figures looked much different as the US accounted for a full third of the world's GDP, still with 6% of the population.

And by 1960, the US still accounted for about 30% of the world's GDP.

These boom years were fueled by a convergence of factors. First, the soldiers home from the war had an easy time in the

'50s finding jobs. Many went to college on the GI Bill. Marriage and household formation took off.

And then there was the high birth rate; in the 1950s 29 million Americans were born, a birth rate equivalent to India—the baby boom generation.

The household growth drove the explosion of the suburbs. Prior to the end of WWII, there had never been more housing starts per year than 620,000. But in 1946 there were just over 1 million and the average housing starts during the 1950s were almost 1.5 million units per year. And with that 1.5 million houses were the same number of stoves, refrigerators, carpets, plus furniture, small appliances, washers and dryers.

One appliance was particularly important, the newest appliance—television. Americans were purchasing them at the rate of 230,000 per month by 1950 and three years later, two thirds of the households had at least one TV.

Companies would never be the same

The companies comprising this economy grew at remarkable rates also. General Motors, the largest company in the country, had sales of $7.5 billion in 1950. By 1959, sales had grown 49% to $11.2 billion.

The first year of the Fortune 500 was 1955. The smallest company included was Copperweld Steel with sales of $49.7 million, a small company today. They employed 3,361 people. The sales of the entire Fortune 500 list were $136.8 billion and employed 7.9 million people.

A short five years later, Masonite was the smallest company with sales of $71.8 million, an increase of 44%. The entire Fortune 500 accounted for $197.4 billion, growth of 45% and had 9 million employees. All this in just 5 years.

The Fortune 500

	1955	1960	% Growth
Total Sales (000)	$136,782,913	$197,394,885	45%
Avg. Sales/company (000)	273,566	394,790	
Total Employees	7,857,483	9,052,009	15%
Avg. Employees/Co.	15,715	18,104	
Size of #500 (millions)	$49.7	$71.8	44%

This growth was reflected in the Dow Jones Industrials, which opened in 1950 at 200.13 and closed a decade later at 679.36, an increase of 339%.

As sales grew, employment grew, number of products grew, stock prices climbed. This was a great decade to be in business. Many of the innovations of years past flowered in this decade. The production line was now standard. The supermarket had replaced the independent grocer. While magazines and radio had provided a national audience, the new television medium would take advertising to new heights.

Essentially, the 1950s saw the first time that a market with vast purchasing resources could avail itself of market efficiencies initiated in the twenties: national distribution and national advertising. If you could make it, you could sell it. And that led to very big companies.

Complexity

As the size of companies grew, their complexity grew also. General Motors, already a behemoth by 1930, was the epitome of complexity. Alfred Sloan introduced remarkable changes in the management structure, particularly decentralization, and had adopted changes in measurement and reporting we now take for granted, such as ROI and ROE.

When he became President of General Motors in 1923, the idea of management was strange. Few businessmen had college degrees; college prepared you for higher callings than business.

While Sloan had no choice but to consider and tackle the challenges of complexity due to size, most firms, well into the 1940s had few in management and many people in production. The pyramids were flat. Business was relatively simple and management was not much of an issue.

But business grew dramatically both during the war years and the decades after. No longer were companies making a single product to sell to a local or regional market. Companies had to learn to deal with a multitude of divisions, manufacturing and marketing numerous products to a range of different markets on a national scale, perhaps even internationally.

Complexity in Marketing

Taking your product to market also became more complex. Distributors of products as diverse as bearings and steel were following the lead of the supermarket and forming regional and national chains. In the markets for electronics and appliances, national wholesalers served as the partner between the television and radio manufacturer and the local retailer.

Department stores, stymied by the depression and the war, resumed their expansion from local chains to regional chains.

Sears launched its first credit card in 1953 and aggressively expanded in the US along with Canada and Mexico. By 1969,

Sears boasted that 1/3rd of the population visited a Sears store every week.

Grainger, at the time an electric motor distributor, had 46 branches across the country by 1952.

Mass production, mass distribution and now, in the fifties we had the introduction and quick adoption of the greatest mass media in the world, television. The country took to this new medium with a passion not seen before. Uncle Milty and the Guard-all Shield. That was television.

While it takes an entire book to cover the sociological changes caused by TV, the impact on business is easily summed. In 1950, the 10 largest advertising agencies billed $683 million. By 1960, they billed $1.6 billion, a growth of 235%. Not bad for a few years work. Advertising became big business in the '50s.

While all this growth brought prosperity, the complexity brought management headaches. Many nice small, easily managed businesses had grown to the point that Alfred Sloan had come to in the mid 1920s. They now had to cope with managing.

The MBA

Wherever there's complexity, there's always someone who comes along to simplify. But let's step a little farther back.

In the late 1800s, a new academic discipline arose. The business school. Following in 1900 came the MBA. The business schools were definitely ahead of themselves. Well into the 1930s, the attitude of business toward the college degree was not particularly favorable. You learned on the job.

By the early 1950s, there were 50 schools granting the MBA degree and in 1955 they graduated about 3,300 students, an average of 66 students per school. But by the 1960s, the degree took off, with almost 13,000 degrees granted in 1965, an increase over ten years of almost 400%. By 2002, the business schools graduated more than 120,000 MBAs.

The MBA programs in the early part of the century are best known for their impact on production and industrial management. Frederick Taylor is probably the best known guru of this era as he pioneered operations management, the way to manage the new production line. The 1920s also saw the beginnings of financial management, first adopted at DuPont, followed by General Motors.

But with the remarkable growth of the 1950s came the need for more management. Smaller firms that prior to the war had manufactured one product in one factory and had a sales force focused on a regional market were now an enterprise of several thousand, manufacturing a range of products, sold to a range of markets all national in scope. While the principles of the assembly line had organized the shop floor, how was management going to be organized?

Growth and complexity resulted in managers with portfolio: personnel—soon to become human resources, finance, research and development, and sales. Where 20 years prior there had been a person or two who did these functions, by 1960 there were managers responsible for the performance of departments of people who carried out these tasks.

What a single person had done in the '30s was now a department with management and staff. And as the cadre of managers grew, the challenge of managing the managers grew. What to do? Management became a task—a discipline in itself. The MBA came into its own. And with this came the creation of the professional manager.

Peter Drucker offered the first guidance in his book, *The Practice of Management*, in 1954. Management by objectives—the (in)famous MBOs. While this is such a common-sense concept, and so ingrained as to now be taken for granted, this was a revolutionary idea at the time. For a manager to actively participate in defining his job, what he is to accomplish, the time frame and what resources he needs, was revolutionary.

Then, Douglas McGregor of M.I.T., advanced his Theory X/ Theory Y management approach in 1960. It was not about selling, engineering or production but about how to treat other individuals such that they as a coordinated group perform a defined task. All about motivation. As he continued to develop his theories, he coined the term, professional manager.

The MBA had gained gold-plated legitimacy. The professional manager could manage anything. It was about people and motivation. You did not have to be a great engineer or a great sales person to be a great manager. Come get your MBA and you, too, can be a professional. And this was just what the increasingly complex and growing businesses needed.

The Birth of Marketing

The 1950s were the decade of the first stirrings of modern marketing. Prior to WWII, all but the largest companies sold into one market and focused on one geographic region. This changed dramatically by the early 1950s. Companies now typically sold:

- Multiple products
- To multiple markets
- Nationally
- From multiple factories

Management now had to cope with multiple sales forces, distribution channels, trade shows, advertising media, sales literature, mailings. Thus was born the marketing manager. Someone had to manage all this and, what with television and other national media, what was now a sizable expenditure.

But what was the goal of marketing?

Yes, it was to manage these functions. But what were the objectives? What was marketing to accomplish. Given the paradigm of the past 75 years, factories produced products that salesmen then sold. Marketing was to help the salesman sell.

But a few people had a different idea.

Peter Drucker fired the early shots in his 1954 book, where he introduced this critical idea,

> "There is only one valid definition of business purpose: to create a customer."

This was a shock to those who thought the purpose of their company was to manufacture their product, and an even greater shock to those who thought that the only purpose of business was to make a profit.

Ted Levitt of Harvard Business School, writing in *Harvard Business Review* in 1960 took this basic idea steps further in his article, "Marketing Myopia." His core idea:

> Business will do better in the end if they concentrate on meeting consumers' needs rather than on selling products.

Salesmen were not happy.

What a revolutionary idea. Many businessmen really didn't grasp it. The basic model of business had people who make things and people who sold things. Companies defined themselves by what they made. But these two men, Drucker and Levitt, hammered on the essential idea of marketing:

The firm exists to solve customers' needs.

How strange.

What a strange time to introduce the concept of marketing. During the 1950s and 60s, if you could make it your salesmen could sell it. Yes, GM and Ford fought for market share. But every year they sold more cars and made more money and life was good. The need to change a basic philosophy of business really didn't sink in. But, the two men tried.

Drucker continued to pursue this theme through the sixties but really rammed it home in his book in 1974, *Management: Tasks, Responsibilities, Practices* :

> "It is the customer who determines what a business is. It is the customer alone whose willingness to pay for a good or for a service converts economic resources into wealth, things into goods. What the customer buys and considers value is never just a product. It is always a utility, that is, what a product or service does for him.

> "Because its purpose is to create a customer, the business enterprise has two—and only these two—basic functions: marketing and innovation."

Drucker went on,

> "Indeed, selling and marketing are antithetical rather than synonymous or even complementary.

> "There will always, one can assume, be the need for some selling. But the aim of marketing is to make the selling superfluous. The aim of marketing is to know and understand the customer so well that the product or service fits him and sells itself."

Arthur Miller was just a bit ahead of his time when he wrote "Death of a salesman" in 1949. But the IRS got it right when it ruled that a business without customers is just a hobby.

So What's Happened?

The top guru of management has redefined marketing. It is not about supporting the sales force, it's there to replace them. Has this worked? Let's look at a few examples:

1. In the mid-1950s, market research was a new and exciting science. Ford Motor Company invested an enormous amount of money in what at that time was the largest market research project conducted—motivational research into the purchase of an automobile. This was hailed at the time as a major milestone in marketing, a turning toward the Drucker model. The study took several years and involved hundreds of respondents.

The net of the survey: the direction for the Edsel.

Ouch. Well, that's overstated. The results were apparently very interesting, but then many of them were ignored. What's the problem? Was the research wrong? Why didn't Ford follow it?

2. Spencer Stuart, a leading executive search firm, surveys employment trends in the business world. A key finding—in 2005 the average tenure of a CMO in the top 100 branded companies is 22 months.

Not even a full two years.

Most aren't leaving their position by choice. What's the problem? Are they not managing their resources? Meeting their objectives?

3. J.D. Power and Associates must be the most recognized firm measuring customer satisfaction. They have

been doing this since 1968 and are best known for their automobile customer satisfaction studies. Their studies show that approximately 80% of owners are satisfied with their cars. Not too bad. You'd expect that there'd be a high repurchase rate.

No.

Only 30% of automobile buyers purchase the same brand. What's the problem? Doesn't satisfaction lead to future sales? Should the car companies not worry about satisfaction since it doesn't drive future sales?

4. Every year about 37,000 new products are introduced into the US market. Two years later only about 15 to 20% are still in the market.

Over 80% fail.

Very few companies outside the fashion industry launch products on the basis of only having a two-year life. Enormous amounts of investment go into market research, design, testing, production facilities, marketing and sales. All with the expectation of a great return to the company.

And 80% fail.

Big expenditures. Terrible odds. Yet year after year, the same companies keep on introducing products, following the same practices, the same research projects, the same introductory tactics, and failing, again and again.

What's wrong? Why is failure so endemic? Are new products that difficult?

5. I was consulting with a group of business units of a major Fortune 500 company. The group marketing director and I met with each of the business unit product managers and prepared a detailed budget tied tightly to marketing objectives

and revenue targets. We presented the detailed plan to the group management which, in turn, presented the plan to the corporate management.

Two and a half months later, the budgets came down from corporate finance. The overall budget was up 5%, the two business units that needed—and justified—an increase of 10% received only 5%. One business unit that actually needed less than the prior year received a 5% increase.

Obviously no one in corporate finance was listening.

The entire marketing/product management group was demoralized. What was the problem? Finance had stated they wanted more rationale for budget requests. Could they not read? Didn't they even care?

6. Over dinner, a salesman for a major trade publication related how he had just finished his annual compensation discussion for the upcoming year. His management would have him increase sales by 10%, his goal to reach a bonus was raised accordingly and his commission was deceased 4%.

He then explained to me that in his territory his market share is 65% while their main competitor carries only 22%. He has penetrated every customer in the territory. There is no additional business.

His response to management: if they changed his goals or compensation from the prior year, he will accept the standing offer from the competition. His compensation program stayed the same.

Next to him at the table sat one of the other sales people. He'd had a similar discussion that morning. The direction of management's offer was similar but his market share was only 40%. Management wanted an increase of 20%. And, of course, the commission and bonus were reduced. That was their last and best offer.

A few days later he accepted a much better offer from the competitive publication for the same territory. About 50% of the business followed him.

How could the publisher and sales manager do this? What was their problem? Did they think they could increase sales just by beating on the sales force? Don't customers have a say in the matter?

7. General Motors and Ford have just announced major reductions in force along with many plant closings. They state they must do this to stay in business. General Motors a few decades ago was the crown jewel of American business. As Detroit goes, goes the economy and Detroit in the 1950s and 60s meant General Motors first. Now the two companies are battling to stay out of Chapter 11.

Yes, the labor agreements of the past are a significant part of the problem. But their marketing is terrible. They cannot sell a car without an incentive. If they built cars that earned a higher value from the customer, they might be able to afford their terrible labor contracts. They could a few years ago. Now they can't compete in the marketplace. They make too many cars too few people want.

Mercedes-Benz, BMW and Porsche sell into the same market, without incentives. More expensive cars. Manufactured in one of the most expensive places in the world to have a manufacturing plant, Germany. How can they do it when GM and Ford can't? What's the problem? The domestic manufacturers run surveys, conduct focus groups, advertise heavily, have enormous dealer networks, and can only sell with incentives, and lose money. What are they doing wrong?

8. New Coke. Feeling beat up by Pepsi, Coca Cola engaged in extensive research to develop a more competitive product. But their research failed to anticipate the strength of the relationship between the consumer and Coke.

They found out fast.

Why didn't they know this? Didn't they consider the relationship they'd built up with the market over the past 80+ years?

One last point: in his 1974 book, Drucker emphatically points out that customer service is the indicator of failed marketing. Where are we now? Calling customer service and having to pound through several layers of menus before we talk to a living human, only to find out that that human is out of the country, speaks English as a second language, and is going to charge you $39.95 to answer your question.

We now charge for failed marketing.

Unfortunately, these are just a few examples of what is going wrong with marketing.

Everywhere that marketing management sees its role as managing budgets for trade shows and media, supporting the sales efforts, marketing has failed.

Everywhere the CEO pounds on the VP Sales for a 5% increase, marketing has failed.

Every time a company launches a new product based on a survey, a focus group and a wing and a prayer, marketing has failed.

Everywhere that the VP Marketing is really the VP Sales, marketing has failed.

Jack Trytten

Everywhere a company thinks its business is making widgets, marketing has failed.

In other words, marketing, marketing as defined by Drucker and Levitt, has failed, over and over again.

What's the problem?

Why?

Part 2: Great Marketing and Its Great Failure

Marketing is so simple a concept but so hard to execute. But for those few that have mastered it, they enjoy growth both in good times and bad, consistent profits, and the envy of the business community.

But so few really understand.

You see evidence every day:

> When you see a commercial that is a turn-off
>
> When you call customer service and pound through a complicated menu only to endure a lengthy wait and you finally reach someone who really doesn't care
>
> When you open the e-mail telling to find that your product support has expired unless you purchase a new upgrade

When you receive multiple mailings the same day from competitive companies offering you something you really don't need

When you enter the store and the salesman's first question is whether you're going to buy today or not

And on

And on . . .

But in the next few chapters we focus on what marketing was really meant to be and what its greatest failure has been.

Chapter 2

What Is Marketing and What It Is Not

Sure, we all know what marketing is. Right?

Wrong. There are true marketing companies, there are companies that do marketing things, and there are companies that don't pay any attention to marketing until their competitors eat their lunch.

Let's compare a simple B2B example. We'll return to a much more complicated consumer products example. These two B2B competitors have an uncomplicated marketing paradigm with no distribution, large customers with very specific functional needs and easily apparent purchase criteria. This straightforward example clearly demonstrates the difference between the two competitors:

The first company, "A", began life making cold-headed parts, mostly fasteners sold primarily to the automotive industry. They were extremely skilled at managing their plant. Their quality was excellent; they provided six sigma before the manufacturing world ever heard of it. They rarely were even hours late on a delivery. Detroit loved them. Superb quality coupled with spectacular delivery reliability. Detroit asked them to do more.

They expanded into precision metal stampings, then assemblies and business grew at a nice steady pace. Profits were good. Not huge, but good, solid and healthy—as long as Detroit was healthy.

The company structure was straightforward:

A significant manufacturing/production department, supported by the following groups:

> Purchasing
> Engineering
> Logistics
> Tooling
> Shipping
> Sales
> Marketing
> Accounting
> Human resources

And, of course, top management

Their business was uncomplicated; they made small parts and sold them. Their sales efforts were straightforward; they called on the purchasing agents, picked up part drawings, submitted bids and most often got the order.

Now let's look at another company that from the outside is not dissimilar: ITW Shakeproof. This ITW division was created to manufacture and market the twisted-tooth lockwasher. Automotive companies were the prime market.

A curious ITW engineer toured an automotive assembly plant and noticed people doing nothing but putting Shakeproof lockwashers onto screws which were then carried over to the production lines. Aha.

The engineer had a flash of insight: put the washer on the screw prior to rolling the threads, thus locking the washer onto the screw. This eliminated the manual assembly step and assured the auto maker that the correct lockwasher was on every screw. The SEMS® was born.

Having been through the manufacturing plants of both company "A" and ITW Shakeproof, I can assure you that A's manufacturing skills were the equal if not better than Shakeproof's.

But Shakeproof risked an additional investment: the cost of engineers focused on customer problems and new products. In fact, when we first visited Shakeproof, an engineer took us to a large room at the back of the plant. They had three cars in various stages of disassembly. The engineer explained that they regularly purchase cars, take them apart, rebuild them, looking for new ways to make the assembly, easier, more reliable, less costly.

Here are the results:

Shakeproof continues to be a major division of ITW and a key supplier to the automotive industry. They have gone on to invent and market a new product about every five years. And each new product has required Shakeproof risk additional capital on new plant and equipment.

Company A was purchased by a competitor which was then swallowed up in the conglomerate fever of the 1980's, having completely lost its identity, market strength and vitality as the U. S. auto makers lost their vitality.

The Differences between the Two

What Company "A" really provided was not small parts but contract manufacturing. They had to base their success on running their machines better than anyone else. This is a very tough business. As soon as a company comes along with newer machines, or a better tool room, the competitive advantage of "A" is weakened.

ITW built its competitive advantage by helping the automotive engineers figure new and better ways to build cars. They dealt with the engineers, the other company dealt with purchasing agents.

Both companies felt price pressure. Everyone dealing with the automotive industry always feels price pressure. But Company "A" only felt price pressure. That's all they knew; they responded by being even more efficient. ITW felt price pressure also—but they responded by creating new parts that cut the manufacturers' costs while providing good margins. As a result, ITW had better margins, stronger customer ties and a healthier market position.

Company "A" is a "make/sell" company. That's what they do; they make things and sell things. They have limited knowledge of their customers, often calling no deeper than purchasing. They think they solve their customer's problems, meeting customer needs. But in the "needs" department, they are order takers. And when some other company comes along with a better idea, they are gone.

Now consider the second company, ITW. They are focused on their customers and their needs and aspirations.

That's their focus.

Yes, they run an efficient plant. But that is to support their ability to make their customers more successful. Their relationships grow much deeper than purchasing agents, with ITW engineers building relationships with client engineers.

Compare: Make/Sell versus Customer Focus

Make/Sell Company	Customer-Focused Company
Strengths:	
Lower marketing costs	Loyal base of customers
	Continual flow of new product ideas
	Greater margins
Weaknesses:	
Lack of customer loyalty	Potentially higher cost structure
Opportunities:	
Compete on price	Continual flow of new product ideas
Threats:	
Products face potential obsolescence	Are there any?

The Ultimate Threat to the Make/Sell Company

Somebody's going to obsolete your products (it might as well be you). Remember these?

>   Carbonpaper sets
>   Typewriters
>   Telegraph
>   Tape recorders
>   Eight track tapes

Floppy disks
35mm film processing
Vinyl Records
Cassette tapes or even reel-to-reel recorders
VCR's
Windup watches
Television antennas

All gone the way of the horse, buggy and buggy whip.

What's next? The CRT on your desktop computer is just about gone and your TV will look much different a few years from now.

But, you say, these are all advancements based on technology. Yes, they would not have happened without breakthroughs but the deciding factor for success was that the innovation provided value in the marketplace.

History is littered with technological marvels that are dazzling to behold yet have little value.

New products are major risks. About 80% of all new products fail. You get better odds at the gaming tables. But, if like ITW Shakeproof, you have a close relationship with your customers—not distribution, but the person or company that benefits from using your product—you stand a much better chance of success. In fact, the odds turn around.

This is simple. If you are customer-focused, you will know— before you make the investment in R&D, plant, materials, distribution—what those customers want. You'll practice market-driven innovation.

Consider a few examples:

Beta was a superior video tape technology yet VHS became the consumer standard. Better marketing resulted in an easier to use system.

When the rush to the internet started in the early '90s, Compuserve was the leading portal, far ahead of AOL. Then and to this day, users complain about AOL service and its many irritating quirks. Compuserve users don't complain—there aren't any. (Well, this is not entirely accurate since Compuserve is still around; they are a small division of AOL). While Compuserve spent dollars on a better portal, AOL spent money on marketing. Remember those CDs that kept arriving in the mail, or tucked into magazines or in on counters of every computer and office supply store? With the ever-increasing numbers of free hours?

Here is the key: technology and marketing aren't mutually exclusive. The great marketing giants of the buggy whips were undone by the technology of the automobile. But the cars being sold now are from the companies with the better marketing.

It was marketing insight that led to the minivan and SUV. Better marketing insight led to the Japanese invasion of compact cars in the '60s, and it is that same insight that's leading the movement to more fuel efficient cars.

Now put yourself in your customer's shoes

Close your eyes, lean back and recall the last time you negotiated the purchase of a car. Did you feel like the mouse as its being teased by the cat? If you did, you'll understand why car salesmen beat out insurance salespeople for the lowest spot on Gallup's survey of most and least honest occupations. Do you consider this type of selling approach good marketing? Do you trust that dealer? Do you want to refer your friends there? How are you going to feel about taking your car to that dealer for service?

By encouraging that type of sales approach, the dealer has laid out the ground rules for your buying.

This is a win-lose situation. The more the dealer wins, the more you lose. And he's counting on wearing you down.

Unless you're masochistic, this is not a situation you're going to cherish. Do you look forward to your next purchase from that dealer?

What do you want from the dealer? You're committing to one of the largest purchases of your lifetime. And you're purchasing a complicated piece of machinery that is to carry you at high speeds, with thousands of moving parts that must operate perfectly during rain and snow and desert heat for several years. You'll need maintenance and repairs; your new automobile has complexity way beyond what you can manage yourself.

Who are you going to count on for help?

I'd like to count on the dealer; I want a relationship. I will have this car for quite some time. But the dealer is willing to gamble away my loyalty in order to maximize his profits. He sees a transaction when I want a relationship.

As a result, I hate his guts.

Customer Focused ⇨ *Customer Relationship*

The customer wants a relationship. Customers hate bargaining. They like reliability. We are social animals and prefer relationships to adversarial transactions. While there are the exceptions, the marketer with the relationship will win. In the early example of Coke and the introduction of New Coke, The Coca Cola Company didn't appreciate the dimensions of their customer relationship. Boy, did they learn about the strength of their relationship. Consider that; a relationship with Coke. A soft drink. Ignoring that cost them big.

Try as they may, the automobile companies will have meager relationships until they change their dealer structure. GM recognized this with Saturn and instituted a policy to create a non-confrontational relationship.

The customer-focused company understands their customers. They understand the desire for a relationship. The result is that they work hard to establish and nurture relationships.

Two Quick Rules of Thumb

Customers want relationships, which is one reason why . . . .

It is generally, well 99.95% of the time, more profitable to service an existing customer than gain a new one.

To put it another way:

> "You wanna be where everybody knows your name."
>
> Theme from Cheers by Gary Portnoy and Judy Hart Angelo

Another way to look at this

Take a look at Fortune's list of most admired companies (2006).

1. General Electric
2. FedEx
3. Southwest Airlines
4. Proctor & Gamble
5. Starbucks

Business and consumer products and services. A real mix. But they all have a common trait—strong customer loyalty. And they've had it for a long time.

Do you have that kind of loyalty? Would you like that kind of loyalty? As long as you look at every sale as a transaction, forget it. If you beat on your sales force for an additional 3% or 10% or whatever of growth, it won't happen. When you spend your best moments out in the plant rather than with your customers, the customers won't have time for you.

There was a wonderful United Airlines commercial a few years ago. (Yes, United may lead the industry in alienating customers, but it was a good commercial). The commercial opened on a conference room and the CEO was announcing to the senior management team—looked like a relatively midsized company—that they had just lost one of the oldest and best customers. Seemed no one had been in touch with them. So, he announced, they were going to change that. They're all going to start visiting customers on a regular basis. And he then started to hand out tickets to each of the senior managers.

This isn't so farfetched. To draw a straight line connecting the dots:

Customer focus leads to customer relationships which lead to customer loyalty.

Business-to-business or consumer products, the dynamics are the same

There are several important differences between B2B and B2C markets. Most B2C products:

- Are sold through distribution
- Have many more purchasing units—individuals, families—with a lower value per unit
- May require consistency in combination with innovation

Let's take these issues one at a time.

First, distribution puts an additional marketer between the manufacturer and the consumer. It's much too easy for the manufacturer to rely on distribution to lead the marketing efforts. Unfortunately for the manufacturer, this usually leads to enlarged margins for the distributor at the expense of margins for the manufacturer.

At the heart of this situation is that the feedback from the consumer is lost to the manufacturer.

He only hears what distribution wants him to hear, a most unreliable source of information.

Second, when the value of the product is low, and as loyal as the customer may be, the depth of the loyalty may never be terribly high. Consider the loyalty to a soft drink.

You head to a movie. They have Pepsi rather than Coke. You want a soft drink to go with the popcorn. You're loyal to Coke. But you purchase a Pepsi. Hey, it's just a movie, just one Pepsi. No big deal.

But this willingness to go against loyalty doesn't happen with high-ticket or infrequently purchased products.

Third, the consistency of a product is often more important than innovation. Kraft turned itself inside out trying to remove trans fats from Oreo cookies. They properly felt it critical to maintain the identical taste and mouth feel in the modified formulation.

The consumer with so many grocery products relies on consistency often across a lifetime. You can feed your kids the same Kraft Mac & Cheese from a blue box that your mom fed you, oh those many years ago. But as you grew up and your tastes grew along with you, rather than change the mac & cheese, Kraft introduced an "adult" version, Deluxe Mac & Cheese.

In the consumer products world, the "make/sell" company focuses on their distribution but rarely have much more than cursory knowledge of their consumer. Why should they? The company relies on their ability to make things. Which they then try to sell. Notice how the focus they have is on what they do. Not the customer.

The customer-focused company is continually developing new products, looking for new ways to delight their consumers. Yes, they pay close attention to their distribution, but they see distribution not as an end in itself but as a partner in providing maximum value to their consumers. Their challenge is in acquiring and maintaining an intimate knowledge of their consumer. In the B2B world, manufacturers and consumers are much closer, even when marketing through distribution. For the consumer products company with millions of consumers rather than hundreds or thousands, the task is much more challenging.

But the leading companies do it.

So What Is Marketing?

Well, it's not sales. It produces sales and it can do that very effectively. But you cannot expect to run an ad and generate sales or go to a trade show or mail a flyer and directly generate sales. That thinking is the same as supposing that beating on your sales force will produce long-term growth.

Marketing is the process of creating and building customer relationships that, in turn, produce sales.

The key is that the objective is not sales. Sales are the end result of:

The Customer Relationship

Marketing is about fostering that relationship.

As such, marketing has a whole set of tactical tools, such as:

Advertising
Direct mail
Tradeshows
Presentations
Public relations
Events
Promotions
Giveaways
Sponsorships
Web sites
Blogs
Email lists
Newsletters
DVDs and CDs
Billboards
Bus cards
Conferences
Speeches
Company magazines
Signage
Balloons
Airships
Spokespersons
Product placements
Coupons
Fishing trips
Pens with your name on them
Toasters (used by banks)

Golf balls with logos
Baseball tickets
And so on . . . .

These are all things that marketing may use. And creative marketing people are continually developing new ones. And "make/sell" companies use these tools also—but usually with limited results. But the only reason to use them is to create and foster relationships. None of them, either alone or in combination will consistently generate sales day after day. Yes, a sale will generate immediate sales today. But you can't do that every day—Detroit has been proving that for quite some time. These are only tactics. They are only to get attention, to communicate to customers and those who you'd like to be customers.

More important, marketing is also about:

- How can we make our products and company more valuable to the customers?
- How can we make it easier to purchase our products?
- How can we earn greater loyalty from our customers?

Marketing encompasses all these—the product, how it's distributed, how it's presented to customers, and, of course, the price, but the critical concept is:

Marketing is the entirety of a set of coordinated activities and decisions aimed at building and managing loyal customer relationships.

Marketing is a strategic activity, core to your business. Before you consider the tactics, you need to have a coherent strategy for building your customer relationships.

So, should you fire all the sales people?

No! At least not yet. But before we consider the sales people, let's take a closer look at these relationships.

A Small Note about Marketing Companies and Technology Companies

Within the business community, financial analysis, the business press and business academia, there is a general definitional consensus:

> Companies tend to define themselves by one of two different orientations: technical/engineering/process or consumer/customer focused.

> Most B2B companies like to think of themselves as technology driven. Their competitive advantage is based on their technologies and processes; their investment and management focus is on advancing and exploiting those technologies.

> The epitome of technology-focused companies is the info-tech company, based on the exploitation of new computer and internet technology. So many of these companies of the last half of the 1990s failed when they found they had no market for their remarkable technology.

> The consumer packaged goods companies exemplify the customer-focused company. Their technology is often not remarkable; management is focused on consumer insights and changing trends.

> Marketing has wildly different roles in each of the types. Marketing in a technology company is generally focused on supporting the salesforce, while in a customer-focused company, marketing is in charge of developing market definition and insight, the sales force is focused on distribution management and the "customer selling" is the task of advertising, package design and other tactical marketing activities.

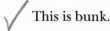 This is bunk.

There are brilliant marketing companies that are focused on technology because the technology of their business is changing so rapidly. Consider Intel, Apple and many of the bio-medical companies. There are also technically brilliant companies that could perform much better if they had some clue as to what marketing is all about. In essence, their technology is saving management's butt because it's covering one marketing mistake after another.

And there are plenty of brilliant marketing companies with little technological sophistication—in a high-tech sense. Consider Starbucks, which, with a wonderful yet almost obvious consumer insight, has reinvented the coffee industry right under the nose of three of the most successful consumer marketers, Kraft (Maxwell House), Nestle and Procter & Gamble (Folger's).

At the same time, to dismiss well-known consumer products companies as low-tech is condescending or naïve. If you have doubts, head for a tour of an automotive assembly plant. Compare the engine compartment of a 1966 Mustang with its recent clone, a 2007 Mustang. Take a tour of a large food processing plant, a soft drink bottling plant or the Fedex distribution center in Memphis. There is high tech here, and that technology is critical to the success of these very competitive businesses.

The primary point is this: marketing and technology are not either/or factors. To succeed in the long term, you need excellence in both.

Chapter 3

Customer Satisfaction, Customer Loyalty and the Customer Relationship

The business world, always up for a good new fad, jumped on quality in the '80s. What Demming had done for the Japanese, any one of hundreds of quality gurus could do for you. The foundation of the quality story, particularly with Philip Crosby, was the need to identify customer expectations and meet or exceed them thus reaching the holy grail of quality:

Customer satisfaction.

And if you are a serious, well-run business, you are conducting customer satisfaction studies on a frequent and regular basis.

Overnight, hundreds of firms sprang up specializing in the appropriate conduct of customer satisfaction surveys. If you have any inclination to compete for the Malcolm Baldridge Award, you had better have a clear history of customer satisfaction surveys to demonstrate how you've improved your quality and exceeded your customers' expectations.

It was not until well into the '90s that a few cynical CEOs scrutinized their customer satisfaction scores and realized that the score had nothing to do with sales, margins, profits, market share or anything else other than the profitability of the "Quality assurance" industry.

Customer satisfaction? Bunk!

This is not to say that quality is not important. It is. Absolutely critical. And the quality movement of the '80s was an important turning point in business. The problem was that one of the key measures, customer satisfaction, was off. Customer satisfaction had little correlation to future sales. Customer dissatisfaction predicted with remarkable accuracy that your sales were going into the tank. But a high level of satisfaction didn't mean your sales would head through the roof. In fact, it didn't even mean your sales would stay level. The reasons?

First, the bar is set too low.

Customer satisfaction is a big "so what." Yes, I'm satisfied, but I would like to be delighted. Ecstatic. Thrilled. In those most sterile of terms, "exceed my expectations."

Second, the bar is set in the wrong place.

In fact, no matter where you set the bar, it's in the wrong place. My expectations for this purchase do not necessarily bear a relationship to my next purchase, unless I am disappointed. My desires change. Needs change. Tastes change.

Consider a friend of mine. He loves sports cars and after college bought a tricked-out Nissan Z. Great car, fun to drive. Then he married, moved to the suburbs and needed a "family" car. His wife hated driving the "Z". Her new second car turned out to be a Chevy Monte Carlo.

But suburbia really got to him and he traded the Z for a station wagon. Needed to haul lumber for the new deck and mulch for the garden. And then came the children, three of them.

So he traded in the wagon on a van for her. And the Monte Carlo turned into a new Lexus for him. But his wife came to loath the van which was a dog to park and he, of course still loved the memory of his old Z car.

So when the mini-van came along, the van was gone in an instant. And then there was a little bigger one, with removable seats, then one with a tape deck and CD player and a power sliding door on each side.

When the oldest child came of age to drive, along came a small Ford for the soon to be three new drivers in the family. And his wife commandeered a new Lexus SUV while he went for his dream, a Mercedes 500 SL.

He was satisfied with each of his cars, with the exception of the van. But by the time he was ready for a new purchase, his needs had changed. His situation had changed. He wanted something new. A customer satisfaction study could not uncover what he might purchase next. He didn't even know. So, what should we marketers do?

Customer loyalty

So now that customer satisfaction has been trashed by the gurus, this is the new grail:

I want loyal customers.

A loyal customer will return to me again and again. Right?

Once again, this depends on how you define customer loyalty. All too many marketers and CEOs define loyalty as buying from me again and again. This is not helpful. This is a circular definition. Why are you loyal? Because you purchase from me again and again. Why do you do that? Because you're loyal.

Here's the conundrum: how are you going to sell me the same thing as you sold me before when my needs, wants, taste and desires have changed in the meantime. Are you thinking that my loyalty to you will result in my purchasing something from you that no longer meets my changed wants? Why? Just because you're you?

Surely you jest. Tiffany's doesn't even pull that off.

Here's the solution. You have to anticipate my changing needs, wants, taste and desires. You have to be committed to that.

Perhaps you feel that's too difficult?

There are quite a few companies—wildly successful companies—who are doing this on a regular, continual basis.

They accomplish this by establishing a relationship with their customers. This is not a "Harvey McKay Relationship" where you know the spouse's name and the kids' names and ages and what sports they like and what kind of restaurants they patronize.

No, the most successful companies make a commitment to make their customers' lives better tomorrow than they are today. This commitment forms the basis of the relationship.

The Customer Relationship

I hope this doesn't bother you but whoever does the laundry in your household may have a close relationship with Procter & Gamble, particularly if they use Tide.

Understanding the relationship between the consumer and the product or company can be challenging. It's subtle. This is not a great affair of the heart, not "As the World Turns," but a relationship built on the consumer's changing expectations and the ability of the marketer to continually advance them.

For simplicity, consider Tide.

Improved. About every year or so, out comes an improved Tide. It usually doesn't cost more unless they have added bleach or a softener. The improvement is not something they just dreamed up in the lab and thought they could sell but the result of a continual process of staying in close touch with consumers to understand their changing needs.

How have washers changed? Have you changed when or how you do wash? Are there stains that don't seem to come out? Are you washing with more cold water? How is your family reacting to your washing? And are your clothes of differing fabrics? And so on . . . .

P & G is continually in contact with their consumers looking for ways they can be of more help. But it is the first step in a process to continually improve their relationship with their consumers. Is it prefect? No, but when you talk to their loyal users you'll find out that it's better than anything else. And those consumers expect that P&G will keep it that way. The consumers count on it. That's the crux of the relationship—for Tide.

Change is a critical factor but you must understand the customer to understand what to change. With Coke, the relationship is built on "refreshing." That is their promise to their consumers as it has been since the 1920s. And they try to deliver on that no matter how you want it or where you are. But as they so rudely found out about 20 years ago, don't change the product. People are loyal to that original taste. But even now they still encompass change—Vanilla Coke, Cherry Coke, Caffeine-free Coke, Diet Coke, Caffeine-free Diet Coke, and so on. That change provides variety but without changing the brand promise of refreshment. Or the original taste.

And McDonald's. They have realized over the years that if they are to continually grow they must offer new menu items. Chicken strips and sandwiches, breakfast burritos, salads and more. But they also realize that the original hamburger must taste the same in every store in the world, the way it tasted the first time you ate one. Change of taste, never. Change of menu—continually.

Yes, you say, easy for them. I make an expensive technical product, costing thousands of dollars, purchased after careful testing and examination. Well, the same can be said of GE's MRI machines, S & C's switchgear for electric utilities, engineered fasteners from ITW, and a host of technical products. What do these companies do? They stay very close to their customers. They build relationships that allow them to gain the knowledge base to anticipate their customers' needs. They don't stop with purchasing agents but work to build relationships with the technical people who use their product.

Take a closer look a GE Healthcare. Given a wakeup call with when competition introduced the first CT Scan machine, GE was not about to be caught again. They introduced the first practical MRI machine but didn't stop there. If they were to maintain their leadership in x-ray equipment, they needed to think and act differently.

GE refocused from making and selling machines to their current direction of aiding the doctor in diagnosing and treating disease and injury. This has led them in directions far beyond the machine world, such as diagnostic pharmaceuticals and education.

They are now organized by medical specialty focused on working with medical researchers and practitioners as they seek to aid the doctor in advancing diagnostic medicine. To keep themselves in close contact with the profession, each practice area has standing panels of doctors that regularly meet to discuss challenges and advancements in their areas.

Staying close to your customers can be considerable work. But it keeps GE far ahead as it meets its continuing commitment to medical professionals.

That is a customer relationship.

It's defined by a commitment on the part of the marketer to make the life of the customer better.

The hallmark is change. The company recognizes that change in the customer is a given. The relationship company cherishes that change as an opportunity to build more loyalty.

The relationship company looks for change, celebrates change and is willing to change. All to better meet changing customer needs.

The Make/Sell Company and Customer Relationships

The make/sell company typically has few real customer relationships. They are process driven, focused intently on how they manufacture and sell.

I was talking with a young turk who had recently joined such a company. Oh, he had so many new ideas, new approaches, new thinking. And the company slowly, firmly beat the creativity out of him with comments:

> We tried that and it didn't work.
>
> We've never done it that way.
>
> I'd be very careful if I were you.
>
> This is how we do it here.
>
> You're kidding me?

And the Young Turk eventually has to face a choice—find a new job or lose his creative drive. The make/sell company has found a way to do business and no one is willing to take the risk to change.

They focus on competition. When competitors come out with a new improvement, they come out with one. Or lower their price. Or both. And slowly, but surely, their margins contract, thinner and thinner.

And then one day, it all disappears. Consider the company supplying screws to the auto companies before ITW Shakeproof came along. They were probably a nice group of people, working hard, making good screws. Then Shakeproof developed the idea to supply their lockwasher on a screw and the prior company's screw business was gone.

Gone. Not coming back.

The copier killed the carbon set.

The iPod has killed the Sony Walkman

Word processing software and the computer killed the typewriter.

The Bowmar Brain killed the old adding machine and Victor Comptometer

Ford killed the buggy whip.

Digital cameras are killing film processing

Dish antennas and cable is killing the old TV antenna just as the old picture tube will be killed by solid state screens.

Change is going to happen. Count on it. You have a choice. You can strive to build relationships with your customers and drive change or you can try to preserve your way of life and hope change is something the next guy has to worry about.

To sum:

Customer relationships are built on your commitment to the future well-being of your customer.

The implications:

> **You will embrace change**
>
> **You will be close to your customer**
>
> **Or (you know what comes next) you'll fail.**

Chapter 4

The Failure of Marketing

Every time we speak to groups, we ask them for their #1 business priority. For CEOs it's:

Growth

We've then offered them four alternatives for organic growth:

1. Sell more existing products to your current customers
2. Sell existing products to new customers
3. Sell new products to current customers
4. Sell new products to new customers

Decisive, they prefer a combination of several. But asked what programs are in place to reach their growth goals, they usually fall back on the same strategy, "trying harder."

For each growth alternative, there's an even harder question:
Why should your existing customers buy more?
Who are these new customers?
Why should existing customers or even new ones buy your new product?

We hear very few answers.

How can these CEOs have any expectations of growth when they have little idea of what new customers, or what new products, or why even the existing customers should buy more?

So they'll try harder, like Avis. We've worked with too many companies where the sales group puts their forecast into the plan only to find that their goal has been doubled or tripled by management in the final plan. Where are these sales to come from? Management doesn't know and the sales force knows that management doesn't know.

If these CEOs expect growth, they had better put together a plan. (Their competitors might have one.)

The CEOs' second priority is loyal customers. Since we started our surveys, the CEOs continue to focus on the critical need for customer loyalty. Yet, when asked what programs and initiatives they rely on to create customer loyalty, they fall back on tactical efforts. So they try a little of this, a bunch of that, but then they cut expenditures for customer service and marketing. Boiling it down, most have no strategic program for building customer loyalty.

Many CEOs don't even know what it means. They confuse "loyalty rewards" for loyalty. Take the airlines. You may fly a particular airline for mileage credits but are you really loyal when they deliver poor service, delays, crowded seating and lost luggage? No, not me. I may fly them for the credits but I don't really like them, much less feel any loyalty. When someone comes with a better offer, I'm gone.

Or consider this item high on the list of customer pet peeves—customer service. Little can stir anger than to have a problem, only to call customer service, pound through multiple menus, only to be put on hold. No wonder why customer service has high turnover. The system itself creates anger. Consider that anger and loyalty don't usually go together. Can a CEO with this kind of customer service really be concerned with customer loyalty?

Then, how's this for building customer loyalty: when companies try to force sales by withdrawing support for older versions of their products. They can't be too concerned about customer loyalty. They can't give me good reasons to upgrade, so they just "give" the withdrawal of their loyalty to me unless I send them more money.

Consider this example. Scott Cook is proud of the customer focus at Intuit. Just what he is so proud of? I purchased Quickbooks in 2003 and shortly after that subscribed to their payroll service which provided up-to-date versions of payroll tax tables. These allowed the program to automatically determine the correct payroll taxes to withhold as I paid salary. This was not cheap.

The program itself costs $200. Not insignificant but not huge, either.

The payroll subscription is an additional $200 per year.

The program with the payroll is really a great program. You just enter the gross amount of pay per period and the program automatically figures out all the taxes. When it's time to pay, the program figures out the appropriate check amounts. And the program continually updates the tax tables to make sure you're withholding and paying the correct amounts. Wow. This is great.

Here's the catch.

In 2005 Intuit informed me they were no longer supporting Quickbooks 2003. Just two (2) short years later. Automobile companies generally keep parts on hand for models ten years old. There are planes flying in commercial fleets that are 25 years old. But Intuit feels two years is plenty. And other than the 30 days after you install the program, they charge for the service call.

Talk about planned obsolescence.

This is taking it to new lows. But they come out with a new version every year and this only promotes their sales.

Hey, no big deal; I don't have to buy the upgrade. Right? No, wrong. Because they do not offer the tax tables on versions they no longer support. So if I want the payroll service, I have to purchase the new program.

Boy, did I become a non-supporter of Intuit in a hurry. Figure it this way. The payroll service costs $300 a year with a free program every two years. And you must have a new program whether you like it or not.

I still do not need any of the enhancements they have offered in versions 2004, 2005 or 2006. I just don't need them. Intuit obviously doesn't care. Instead, they are willing to pass up the subscription of $200 for the payroll service because I was not willing to drink their Kool-Aid.

And they lost a supporter at the same time.

Do you think their marketing is run by the CFO? Could be.

Bah, CEO! Don't talk to me about your concern for your customer, your need for loyalty. Not when your company treats me this way. You have no concern for your market, your customer. It appears you are solely concerned with sales and profits and meeting projections.

But, most CEOs really do care about their customers. They just don't know quite what to do about it.

The core problem: most CEOs don't have much of a clue as to what marketing is.

Now this shouldn't be a surprise. Most didn't rise to their position with either marketing or sales experience. Less than 20% of the CEOs of Fortune 500 companies have backgrounds with significant experience in marketing. The bulk of them have functional experience in finance and operations, having started their careers in technical positions. And even those with sales experience often don't understand marketing strategy.

Why should they have any skills in marketing when perhaps the only place they studied it was at an MBA program years ago?

Perhaps their CMOs should fill this void with their understanding of marketing. That is, before their 22-month tenure ends.

The Chief Marketing Officer

The Chief Executive should demand—demand—to know what programs are in place to grow the company, to earn customer loyalty. This is the core of the CMO's responsibility. Yet, when our company, Insight Direction, Inc., conducted a study covering the perceptions of marketing across several thousand senior marketing personnel, the results were frightening. We asked them one simple question:

What is your definition of marketing?

Over 60% responded with, "To support sales."

Wrong! Oh so wrong.

Another 30% defined their job as doing marketing activities: running ads, managing trade shows, sending out newsletters, producing catalogs, etc. The implication of their answer, "We don't know why we're doing it, but we're sure doing it well, I guess."

What they don't have is a clue.

So, why are they doing these things? Who else would do them? They perform these functions because the person in their job before them did it.

Less than 5% clearly understood their job as creating and nurturing customer relationships.

Why so few?

The vast majority of all the CMOs in the survey have MBAs. They had to study marketing to get that degree. They should have learned the concept there.

Peter Drucker published his tome on management in 1954, over 50 years ago. Every MBA working today should have read his arguments that the function of a business is to create and nurture customer relationships.

Ted Levitt article "Marketing Myopia" published in 1960 and spelled out this definition of marketing. He came back 20 years later with his book, *The Marketing Imagination*, and went into great detail.

What happened? Were these CMOs, all of them, just not paying attention? Marketing is not a new concept.

My guess: they joined their company out of graduate school and found that marketing as they were taught wasn't practiced. That wasn't the way things were done. The old culture was too strong. And by the time they became CMO they'd forgotten.

Marketing arteriosclerosis had set in long before they even came to the company; process and procedure took seniority over customer relationships. All too often their choice when faced with a marketing decision was to do it the way it's been done—or find somewhere else to do it.

They're doing what the guy before them did, hopefully a little better. So they go along and after 25 years of old habits they find themselves the CMO. By then it's tough to change.

If the CMO can't manage a real marketing organization, you can't expect the CEO to do it.

When the CFO wants to trim expenditures—which they should be doing continually—by tightening the screws on the customer service costs, where is marketing? Are they making the case that this angers customers who then go elsewhere? The loss in revenue outweighs the savings. Who stands up for the customer?

Where's the CMO when management decides that the sales goal should be twice what the sales department put in their forecast. It's the only way the numbers work out so management can "earn" their bonus.

Where is the CMO when the sales manager routinely reorganizes sales territories to keep the selling costs low? Who's sticking up for the customer who had a strong relationship with that sales person?

Where is the CMO when the CFO's financial plan rests on a top line that's significantly more than current customer relationships can provide?

Where is the CMO when management forgets that distribution is there to add value to the customer for your product but instead considers them the enemy?

This is the company with marketing so bad you'd expect them to go out of business. I wish.

The worst examples are so many software companies, who just don't get the importance of customer service. They think it's a profit center. If they had easy to install products, if they had decent manuals, if their products didn't conflict with so many other common programs, then, perhaps, they wouldn't need customer service. But when it's a profit center, why do anything that would harm that revenue stream?

And the CMO is all too often the one who creates all the bogus little fees and hidden charges that alienate customers. What are they thinking?

If anyone in a company should understand the role of marketing, it must be the CMO first. They shoulder the responsibility.

So what's the biggest failure of marketing?

The real failure of marketing, the worst failure, the critical failure:

> Marketing hasn't convinced the business world how critical marketing—real marketing—can be to the successful growth of the company.

The first failure of marketing is to itself. Marketing hasn't sold itself.

Too many CEOs don't understand.

Too many CMOs don't understand either. But they should.

Can Your Company Be Successful Without Successful Marketing?

What a silly question. The answer is obvious. There are hundreds—perhaps thousands of companies that tell us so.

Sure you can!

In a manner of speaking.

You have sales and customers, don't you? You sold more this year than last. You have industry experience, intuition, history and a basic idea how to grow.

Perhaps you do some market research, focus groups and surveys. Good customer satisfaction scores.

So many companies just go along like this and life is good.

In fact, you are marketing in a sense. You have delegated your marketing to either your sales force or your distribution. They are the ones who are trying to create and nurture your customer relationships. They are doing it without you, without your planning, without your control.

That's fine. But this can become problematic—and very expensive.

When the smart sales person leaves, the customers leave too. Sooner or later.

When the distributor wants more margin, you'd better go along or his customers will go with him.

> The sales person or the distributor owns the customer relationship not your company. If there is any loyalty at all, it has little to do with you.

Consumer packaged goods companies found this out over the past twenty years. They tried to buy sales and share with coupons and promotions. They neglected the customer and didn't notice their brands were losing value and loyalty along with it.

The grocers took over. Now they rule the roost. They own the customer relationship. Think about your own habits. Will you go to another store just because your favorite store discontinued your brand of hotdogs? Probably not. Where's your loyalty?

So to keep distribution you pay the fees, cut your margin and keep your sales volume while the distributor keeps the profits. The grocers added one fee after another, slotting, promotional, display and so on, all coming out of the manufacturer's margin.

To build back profits, manufacturers turn to the promise of new, exciting products. These new products will have great margins and with current products under competitive pressure with little customer loyalty, you shift your focus to a new product or two.

But where do the new product ideas come from?

Now you rely on your technology group and occasional management inspiration for new product ideas. The ideas are rarely frequent enough and often fail when they get to the market. Without a solid customer relationship, an intimate relationship, developing new products is like throwing darts in the dark.

That bullseye is small, very small.

What will the market consider so important they'll change their ways? It must offer significantly greater value. And the market defines what's important, what's value—not you.

Finally, you are subject to the biggest threat of all—someone will make your product obsolete. Then where will you be? A factory with no sales. Another cover story for *Ridicule* magazine.

Sure, the marketing company can suffer the same fate. But their focus on creating and nurturing customer relationships, building customer loyalty should have them focused on creating new products for their customers. They are usually the ones leading the others.

Yes, you can be successful without marketing, only until a marketing company comes along and eats your lunch.

So a marketing company will always win over one that's not?

Not necessarily.

There are many companies that think they really are marketing companies. How many companies have a mission statement that places a priority on the customer? Almost every one I've seen.

Those that sincerely consider themselves marketing companies try to live up to that mission. They conduct regular focus groups among their customers. Surveys frequently follow, trying to learn what their customers think. They may even have customer advisory boards.

They spend significant dollars on customer service. Stay close to their distributors. They put heavy resources against sales training. Their marketing expenditures are the largest line item on their income statement.

And if they are in a technology-driven market, they spend heavily on R&D. New products, new processes, all designed to give their customers a better product.

But they fail. And the failure is usually the same.

> A transaction is more important than a loyal customer.

All the good intentions and hard work at a corporate level fail to make it to that critical interface when the customer is ready to buy. Cut every cost. Get every dollar that you can. Maximize the profits of every transaction.

Who can think of relationships at a time like this?

We worked with a company that truly wanted to take a strong marketing approach with their customers. It was a new company with strong backing from their corporate parent.

They were in a market with heavy competition and a product that appeared to be a commodity. Every competitor was selling on price. But the customers needed more than the commodity—there was a terrific opportunity to sell service along with the product that would pull the company far above the others and allow for premium pricing.

However, this meant that the company had to have sales personnel trained to sell the service with the product.

They couldn't implement this. They knew how but they couldn't discipline themselves to go to market radically different than competition.

They are no longer in business.

Good intentions. Poor implementation. And companies that had no clue about marketing killed them off.

Since then two startups took the same marketing approach, implemented it well and are now driving the market.

You can't just want to be a marketing company and go through the motions.

You have to follow through. Implement. Do it well.

Marketing is hard work. It requires immense discipline. If you're going to harness the power of marketing, you have to:

- Have a great product
- Promote it well
- Manage your channels efficiently
- Price your offering appropriately
- And focus on your customer relationship

There are so many critical decisions and you have to make most of them correctly.

Let's take a look at some failures and how you can avoid their mistakes.

One last thought: What if . . . .

What if you were the only company in your industry driven by marketing?

What if one of your competitors is focused on marketing—and you're not?

Part 3: Strategy and the 4 P's

Every Introduction to Marketing course teaches basic marketing strategy, and then the tactical 4 P's: Product, Place, Promotion and Price.

Why do so few understand?

Michael Porter has spent the better part of twenty years simplifying the basics of strategy. And without strategy, the tactics, those 4 P's, mean nothing but failure.

And there's so much confusion. Companies striving to be customer-centric, meaning they want their customers to become focused on their product.

The failure of so many new products with such a waste of resources.

The irritation we all have so often with so many companies is that they are just trying to do one simple thing: make a lot of money for themselves.

Here we focus on what strategy should mean to marketers, and then take a very close look at the many ways companies attempt to snatch defeat from the jaws of victory through their tactical execution.

Chapter 5

The Critical Importance of Strategy

Building customer relationships. Seems straightforward. But before you dive into tactics—like reinvigorating the newsletter and finding someone to manage a blog, you need a strategy. Building relationships is not a strategy. Nor is being the low cost producer or having low turnover or being the industry ROI leader. Those are goals, good things to do perhaps, but they are not strategies. Take a look at a few companies and their strategies.

Southwest Airlines and Midwest Airlines both have different business models than the traditional hub and spoke carriers. These two carriers do things differently from each other and the traditional carriers. One has no meals while the other has gourmet meals. One has all coach while the other has all business class. One targeted the price conscious traveler, initially the individual traveling on personal business, while the other targeted the business and leisure traveler wanting a more upscale experience. Up until the end of 2001, they were the only two consistently profitable airlines in the country. Both have expanded rapidly over the past four years, running counter to the rest of the industry.

They had two similarities:

> They both were operationally excellent
> They both had solid, well-defined strategies

Neiman Marcus and Wal-Mart, both have well-defined strategies and both are successful. Consider the most admired companies—all have well-defined strategies.

What it is and what it is not

Six Sigma is about operational excellence as are MBOs, controlling costs, maximizing revenues, TQM and most of the management initiatives of the 1980s and 90s. This was the challenge presented by the Japanese. They were operationally spectacular. Every business should strive for operational excellence. But, that is not strategy.

Strategy is about being different—choosing different operations and being successful through those choices. Southwest has a different strategy than the traditional carriers as does Midwest. Southwest targeted a different market that had consistent values and they focused on serving it. Midwest did the same, just with a different market.

As Michael Porter stated in his article, "What Is Strategy," in the *Harvard Business Review,* (Nov.-Dec., 1996),

The Failure of Marketing

"Strategy is the creation of a unique and valuable position involving a different set of activities."

In his book, *Competitive Strategy*, (Free Press, 1980), Porter goes on to define three generic strategies:

Quality
Quality focused on a niche market
Low price

Generally, the first company into a market is focused on quality. Many large companies targeting mass markets are focused on this also. To a great degree they are able to define what quality means because they are the first.

By the time there are several companies in a market for any length of time, the best way for them all to survive is for several to target niche markets and become the quality leader for that niche. Thus, Sub Zero is the quality leader for the high-end refrigerator market.

And it seems that every market has its price leader.

These are generic categories. Each firm has to create its own specific strategy within its niche.

Consider these two companies we worked with a few years back. ITW Shakeproof, mentioned in Chapter 2, works closely with customers to help them with better ways to assemble their products. Imaginative, creative and quite profitable. They have significant investment in R&D, a large engineering staff and highly trained sales force.

Company "A" also made fasteners and sold to the same customers. They did little R&D related to developing new products but were tenacious in looking for more efficient ways to make fasteners. But they had little investment in marketing and their sales force was much less technically astute. They didn't have to be. The company was also quite profitable.

The two companies were quite successful at how they pursue their market.

Strategy is about choices and commitment. Choose your target. Understand their values. Then target your business to maximize the value you can deliver while minimizing your costs.

But you have to put your stake in the ground.

You have to commit. You cannot be all things to all people. Are you going to serve a premium market? Are you the "Tiffany" of your business? Understand how much of the market will pay a premium for this kind of service. Estimate how much it will cost you to supply that service. Can you make money? What will you be able to earn serving a different segment? Where will you commit?

Shakeproof has chosen to lead their customers. They have close relationships with both the design engineering and manufacturing engineering groups. They spend an inordinate amount of time in the assembly plants. All of their products are patented. They have an experienced in-house group of patent attorneys. They spend considerably on new product R&D. They have a strategy of helping their customers succeed

Company "A", on the other hand, made different choices. While they aren't particularly close to design engineers, they were very close to the manufacturing groups and purchasing. They have a larger logistics group than ITW and were practicing JIT before the Japanese. They had computerized order, inventory and production flow activities early on and had a robust manufacturing R&D program. They could make product quickly and at a very low cost.

What was their strategy? Low cost.

They are operationally excellent. That's not a strategy. We all should strive for this excellence. But to the auto companies, they are just another bidder, another fastener and small parts supplier. Their value proposition is one of price and delivery. There are many other parts suppliers like this. They make things and sell them.

Marketing Strategy

If strategy is about how you do business differently, marketing strategy is about how your marketing strategy differs. And, given that a business is a system composed of interdependent functions, marketing being one of them, if your marketing strategy is different from your competitors, other parts of your business are most likely different also. Marketing strategy can't be developed in a vacuum.

Another example, two plastic resin manufacturers. Competitors, to a degree. They both make the same type of resin. But one has a sales force of 140, costing an estimated $14 million or more, serving a large number of smaller customers. They also need to supply a significant amount of technical support as their customers are not particularly savvy. They spend very little on advertising and promotion, attending a few trade shows and little else. They have a relatively fixed number of grades of resin available in a variety of quantities.

The second company has a much smaller sales force of 30 people costing about $4.5 million. The sales people are all engineers and each services a few huge customers. They spend an additional $3 million on sales support activities. All resin is produced to order with properties tailored to the particular customer and shipped in tank cars.

The dollar sales for both companies are almost identical and the profits very similar. Both have very efficient operations but tailored specifically to meet the differing needs of their markets. They chose different business targets with differing values and designed their activities to maximize the value to their target.

While they both make the same product they really don't compete too much. One has focused on serving the small, relatively unsophisticated customer who needs technical help; the other targets the large customer, sophisticated and needing specialized grades of the resin. They are in different businesses. Their different strategies required different marketing strategies with one relying heavily on sales coupled with heavy technical support, the other focused on sales efforts directed at intimate relationships with customers.

Your strategy

What are your strategy alternatives? Which alternative is right for you? It's a difficult decision. But if you don't make it you will most likely end up without a strategy: no one to nobody.

And you might as well forget a marketing strategy. Without an overall business strategy your target market is whoever will buy and you are just the company pushing a product into a market. You're not concerned with meeting needs.

You may be in business today but tomorrow, the company with a strategy will run you down. Just as Southwest is doing to the traditional carriers, just as the airlines as an industry did to the railroads, just as the foreign car manufacturers are doing to the American auto industry, just as Sony did to the American electronics industry, just as . . . well, you get the idea.

And as for tactics

Your sales force, distribution, advertising, direct mail, pricing policy, and all the other tactical marketing decisions, well, you're wasting your time. Who are you talking to? What are you offering them? Why are you special? Why should the market pay attention to you?

Until you have a clearly defined strategy, you can't answer these questions. And without answers, how do you make a decision? Who should the ad target? What should it say? Will that claim make a difference? Probably not.

First, define your target and determine your strategy.

The next great failure of marketing is a result of not having a strategy. As a starting point to avoid that failure, you need to answer the question:

What kind of relationship do my customers want?

And the corollary,

What kind of relationship do I want with my customers?

Answering these questions is not as easy as it may look. But the place to start is with a close examination of your product or your service.

Chapter 6

What product do you sell?
What product do they buy?

The first issue most marketers face is determining what their product should be.

Whoooa there.

What do you mean, what the product should be? You probably already have a pretty good idea of exactly what your product is. In the past several years we've consulted with companies whose products are gymnasium equipment, fasteners, chemicals, athletic equipment, electric motors, plastic film, and concrete panels. They knew exactly what their products were. There. Look at it. Just what do you think it is?

All of them were wrong.

The first set of issues in building customer relationships are related to your product:

> What exactly is your product from the customer's viewpoint?
> How can you add to the customer's value of your product?
> What related products can you offer the customer?

Your customers don't want to buy your product. In fact very few people want to buy any product. People want to buy something else—the product of the product.

The Evolution of the Product

In the early seventies, some very smart marketing (VSM) person pointed out that products had features and benefits. Features were something inherent in the product. For example, a cookie being low in trans fats is a feature of the product. A benefit is what the purchaser gains from the product—once again, the benefit of lower trans fats is lower cholesterol which leads to a healthier cardiovascular system. These are benefits which are results of the product. The product of the product.

This distinction between features and benefits would seem obvious but there are still many marketing people who don't fully grasp the difference between features and benefits.

Then, our VSM person postulated that it was easier to sell using benefits than with features. This became known as benefit selling. Makes sense. Instead of telling people they should buy because of a feature and trust them to figure out what it would do for them, start out by telling them the benefit which is what they really want to buy.

Obvious.

But it didn't work very well. Hardly an improvement. Why?

What about functionality?

As our sales person studies the features of what he is to sell and derives the benefits, he faces a huge problem:

Few products in a competitive market have significantly differing functions.

Why? Suppose you and I are arch competitors. I then discover something remarkably new that provides a spectacular new level of functionality. Ho, ho. You're going out of business as I stomp on you stealing your customers.

But, are you going to just lay there? Probably not. You're going to move heaven and earth to find a way to provide at least the same new level if not an even higher level and retain your customers.

Consider the housewares business. As you travel the long aisles of the Spring International Housewares Show in Chicago, you notice an amazing new idea. I will guarantee that by Fall, there will be six other companies offering knock-off versions of the new product.

There are only a few exceptions:

> The market is so small it doesn't offer enough in additional sales
> The margin is so tight it doesn't offer competitive air
> The new functionality is protected by intellectual property protection such as a patent.

I have a charcoal grill I purchased specifically because of one function; it has a built-in propane lighter for the charcoal. I prefer the taste of charcoal-grilled food and cook outdoors most of the summer. But I intensely dislike the taste, smell and process of using lighter fluid. This grill provides the ideal answer. It is only made by Weber Stephen, no one else. And there is only one model. I would guess they don't sell many of these, just enough to keep on making them.

DuPont created the Stainmaster process and reinvented the marketing of carpet. While there are many carpets that claim stain resistance, Stainmaster is protected by an array of patents, trademarks and copyrights. There is nothing equal.

But consider how little time it took the other auto companies to introduce minivans after Chrysler created the first one and sales took off. Or how quickly the industry offered SUVs after Jeep created a hit with their Grand Cherokee.

What you typically experience in a market is a variety of competitive products each with enough minor functional differences to provide some distinctiveness but rarely a product with such superior functionality that it dominates a market for any length of time.

This holds true in the B2B markets also. If Klein comes out with a pliers with a bent nose sized to help with a particular task, the other tool makers will introduce similar bent-nosed pliers within months at the longest.

We worked with Ingersoll-Rand on marketing their air compressors. In any given class of machine, each competitor has a comparable unit and each of the manufacturers have "solid independent tests" verifying that theirs is the best compressor. Talk about making life difficult for the plant engineer. There is very little that is significantly different.

So what's our sales person focused on features and benefits to do? He looks over the functions and tries to predict which ones will provide the benefits that will captivate his customers.

But when the competitive products are so similar, what can possibly be that exciting?

If he sells on price, his sales manager may suggest he's pursuing a "career ending" strategy. So he needs to find something else. What could it be?

Functionality vs. "something else"

For the sake of an example, pretend you live in Chicago, were I live. Come the fall you would recognize that you definitely needed a winter coat. So out you go to the stores. There are plenty of winter coats. Consider the differences:

Weight
Length
Fabric
Lining
Construction
Pockets
Hood
Cuffs on the sleeves
Buttons, zippers or both
Removable lining
Fit

Now these are all features and they lead to multiple benefits—you can figure those out. They all deal with functionality—how warm will the coat be, how long it will last, and so forth. Functional benefits.

But there is one benefit that doesn't relate to any one feature—and with some products or services doesn't relate to any of the features.

"Is it me? Does it reflect my personality?"

For your coat, this is the "something else," an intangible benefit. And this benefit usually makes or breaks the sale. There are hundreds, at least, of warm coats. The one you buy is the one that "is you."

So, you're thinking, that's fine for a coat, but I make technical widgets. Consider a company, Precision Plastics. They manufacture plastic parts on contract and pride themselves on their precision. They can, they told us, hold extremely close tolerances.

Their plant is a thing of beauty, no oil stains, no scrap lying around, well lit, spotless floor, organized. Their employees take great pride in what they do. Non-union, well paid, great spirit.

We felt their market strategy a little cavalier. They sent out a beautiful capabilities brochure with personalized letter to purchasing agents and followed up with a phone call. They asked the PA to fax them a blueprint of a part with their requirements and they would fax back a bid.

They had built their business with this casual approach to the market, but it had taken them this far. Now their growth had leveled out. What should they do?

We interviewed a sample of their customers in depth. What we found out shocked our client, particularly the president.

The customers didn't care about precision. Just not an issue.

But they did care deeply about something else. The parts they sent to our client were not critical parts. The tolerances were clearly stated on the print and not overly close. The parts, in fact, were relatively simple, and many companies, the customers felt, could make them. About the only function that was critical was delivery and even then, they usually allowed plenty of time. Very few orders were rush.

So why did they buy—actually show considerable loyalty—to our client?

Because purchasing had come to realize that they could easily fax a blueprint to them, receive a reasonable quote and could count on a definite delivery date. As they explained to us, our client was a dependable, reliable source for simple parts.

So why was this important?

Digging deeper, this allowed the purchasing agent to bid out these parts quickly so he could spend more time on the critical parts and materials.

They were actually selling time. But wait, there's more.

Looking even deeper, the sourcing of critical parts and materials was much more fulfilling than the simple parts sent to our client. They were also selling self-fulfillment.

But there was one last step to the analysis.

The sourcing of critical parts and materials is what could catch management's attention. These were the activities that could move your career ahead—or behind.

> The PA could spend more time where he really felt he could make a difference to his career.

That's Precision Plastic's "something else." Precision had nothing to do with it.

The Product of the Product

It's not uncommon for companies to have little idea of the true reasons their customers purchase their products, or competitor's offerings. Consider the organization of a mid-sized company:

V·√/∿

The Failure of Marketing

CEO

Executive VP

VP Sales and Marketing

VP Sales

Regional Sales Manager

Sales person

Customer

Six levels from the customer to the CEO and with each level a layer of detail, a degree of accuracy is lost.

And the "something else" that drives the actual sales, while obvious once uncovered, is rarely obvious on the surface.

Consider what this is like in a more complicated marketing situation. The company makes equipment for gymnasiums such as basketball backboards, pads, curtains, exercise equipment and the like. They pride themselves on their quality, recognizing that failure of the equipment could result in serious injury of a student.

Their sales manager supervises regional managers who call on their dealers. The dealers do not handle competitive equipment but lines of complementary products that go into new schools such as lockers and case goods. The dealers sell the products on an "installed" basis, managing a subcontractor who performs the installation.

The products are typically sold when a district is building a new school or remodeling an older gymnasium. The first purchasing influence is the person in charge of the design at the school district. The next person to be sold is the architect developing the plan. Finally, the contractor with the winning bid must be sold. Their dealers were excellent at selling the school district's construction manager. The client's emphasis on quality—long life, low maintenance, high reliability—was just what the school was looking for.

Then the dealer had to sell the architect. Schools are usually designed by architects who specialize in school design to the exclusion of other buildings. This is a relatively exclusive group. These architects also preferred our client, supposedly, our client thought, for the same reasons as the school's construction manager.

Finally, with an approved design the project went out for bid. Consider that with public schools the purchasing procedure is usually set by the state. This generally requires bid contracts based on a detailed Request For Proposal, with the lowest qualified bidder awarded the contract. The contractor winning the bid also usually has the option of substituting materials and equipment specified in the RFP if he can convince the architect or the school that the material is "of equal or better" quality.

In other words, the contractor along with the bid procedure redefines the purchase criteria. Now it's "low price wins." This is where our client felt they were losing business. The dealers weren't calling on the contractors, or when they were, they weren't convincing them of the superior quality of the products.

Our client was the quality leader—and the "high-priced spread" in the market. This was not the good place to be when schools were under increasing financial constraints with demands for more service combined with lower funding.

Our client was in a quandary. What to do?

First, they needed to understand the architect and find out what was that "something else." Quality was not an issue with them. A falling piece of gymnasium equipment was an extraordinary rarity. But our client offered something else—a deep bench of engineers who would figure out how to mount the equipment in the gym, no matter what the architect designed.

Simply, they allowed the architect total freedom of design with no constraints for mounting equipment.

To the architect this is huge.

It was really "something else."

And what our client need to communicate to the architect was that if they allowed the contractor to use a less expensive competitive product, that substitution would eventually result in our client not being able to offer the engineering services. Maybe the product was close enough to be considered "or equal" but our client's service to the architect was not.

Second, everyone knows that contractors are cost driven—right? Wrong. Our client had to put a few things in perspective. His total sale per school was about $100,000, a mere drop in the bucket for a $35 million school. The contractor did not seek out the lower priced products but was willing to accept what competition brought.

Our client also needed to understand that from the contractor's viewpoint, the product was one of the last items installed in the school. If it showed up late or missing parts, or the installation subcontractor was late or incompetent, the cost to the contractor would be much greater than any savings from the cheaper product. At this point in the construction, time really was money.

Our client needed to be able to guarantee timely, accurate and fast installation. The installation of their products was one of the few last things standing between the general contractor and his paycheck. To the contractor this was critical. It was their "something else."

The "something else" for our client may seem obvious to you now. But it wasn't to our client or anyone else in the industry until our client went to work on our findings. And for both the architect and the contractor, the "something else" that closed the sale had nothing to do with the functionality of the product.

The direct sales people had a fair idea of the value the architect placed on our client's engineering staff. But by the time this was passed up to management, it was so watered down that management was stunned when we demonstrated just how critical these people were to their sales.

Everyone in the company knew how important delivery and installation were to the contractor. They knew this from those instances when delivery or installation was late. But they hadn't connected the dots. The contractor's severe reaction indicated how important this was to him.

These critical purchase factors were not new. The sales people were not surprised at our recommendations. Yet management had not realized their critical nature until our involvement. The word had not been passed up nor understood by middle management. It wasn't that the sales people hadn't been talking; no one was listening.

Functionality and B2B Products

The functionality of a product is the first reason for purchase. But as noted earlier, unique functionality is short lived unless protected by patents, copyrights or other intellectual property protection.

ITW enjoyed a lengthy period of superiority with SEMS®, their lockwasher and screw, due to the patent. And once it expired, competitors were everywhere.

And then the race is on. How can you add improved functionality? With emerging technologies, significant advances in functionality come quick and in big jumps. Look at what happened to computers from the mid-seventies through 2000. Huge increases in memory, speed and storage. But each increase was slightly less that the previous. Much of the need was driven by improved operating systems and application programs. And their increased functionality was enormous at first but the increases now, twenty years later, are smaller and less compelling.

By 2007 the desktop computer is pretty much a commodity, sold on price. With the few exceptions of heavy game players, graphic artists, engineers running complex CAD programs and a few others, there is little reason to spend more than $500 on a desktop.

So why are people purchasing computers for $1,000 and up? Why are they buying laptops that never move off their desk?

There must be "something else."

ITW still sells a lot of SEMS®, the screw with the lockwasher, and probably at a premium price, even though the patent has expired. Why? There must be another reason.

The core reason the marketing of so many business-to-business products is so frustrating is because differences in functionality have become minor over time and competition. And the search for a competitive edge too often results in a resounding "so what?" from the market. The companies never look to see if there is a "something else," no look beyond the functional.

Functionality and the Consumer Product

If you thought the B2B functionality situation was tough, consumer products put them to shame. The first time I went to the International Housewares Show Water Pic introduced their showerhead with the pulsating jet. Six months later there were four knockoff products.

In more modern times Salton introduced the George Foremen Grill. The knockoffs came; a few survived. Then along came the Panini press; along came the knockoffs. The weeding out of the survivors still goes on. Unique functionality lasts about 6 months with few exceptions. Yet, after the weak copies are driven from the market, several competitors remain.

Consider the ubiquitous automatic coffee maker.

> Cuisinart
> Krups
> Braun
> DeLonghi
> Mr. Coffee
> Hamilton Beach

They all work the same. There are four basic versions;

> Non-programmable with glass carafe
> Programmable with glass carafe
> Non-programmable with thermal carafe
> Programmable with thermal carafe

And each manufacturer has a few specials that the others don't make. But you can be sure if there was significant volume, they'd all be there.

They each work the same. Load the coffee in the filter. Fill with water. The water is heated and boils up to drip into the coffee. Then through the filter and into the pot.

So which one should you buy? They differ primarily in design, although not by much. Black or white with touches of stainless.

Which design looks best?

Which manufacturer do you trust?

One thing's for certain—it's something other than functionality.

Consider the basic functionality of so many consumer products, just the pure functionality. How do they differ?

> Refrigerators
> Washers and dryers
> HD TVs
> Stereos
> Automobiles—by class
> Telephones
> Kitchen knives and gadgets
> Brooms
> Vacuum cleaners
> Hair dryers
> Electric toothbrushes

The products at differing price points have different functionality. But when you take into consideration the price points, the functional differences pretty much go away. So how do you choose? You had better find that "something else."

The Challenge of Food

Wow, what is food?

Functionality is not much of an issue. While the health food segment or those with allergies choose with careful consideration of nutrition, ingredients and related issues, most of us pick something to eat because it sounds like a good idea. Boy, is that ever vague.

The primary issue is taste. And what would taste good right now would taste terrible some other time.

What we choose to eat is affected by sight, smell, texture, mouth feel, along with time of day and meal occasion. But there is more. These factors, along with nutritional benefits are only part of the story. There's more. Food has to be the most difficult product to determine what drives the purchase.

After air and water, it is the most fundamental human need. While it is critical to life, few of us in developed countries worry about getting something to eat. Rather, we worry about what to eat. What would we enjoy?

Our tastes change based on how long it's been since we last ate. Go on a fast. It's amazing what you'll find appetizing on the second day.

So what makes food appealing?

Well, we all know. it's sweet, but then it's not sweet but savory. It's got taste, but then it's subtle. We can go on with this but the key point is straightforward: food is a highly emotional topic, and the reasons we eat what we eat, when we eat are "something else."

Food is all about "something else."

Searching for "something else"

So what is this something else, this product of the product? Sometimes it's actually something functional that you had never considered such as the architect specifying a brand because the manufacturer offers design assistance. This is relatively easy to determine with good market research. But all too often it's not done. It's ignored.

96

The Failure of Marketing

Marketers are all too willing to settle for easy answers: quality, service, price. And then they wonder why they are beaten up in the market.

But then, sometimes "something else" is not a clear functional difference.

It's the dreaded "E" word—it's emotional.

Oh my goodness. If it's emotional, then there is nothing we can do. The buyer is making an emotional judgment.

This is a terrible excuse to do nothing.

Plain and simple, this is a cop-out on the part of the marketing people. You can understand the "emotional" decision.

What this all boils down to:

> The next failure of marketing is that all too often, marketers do not have a comprehensive understanding of what their product really is.

If makes no difference what the product means to you. The only person you need to understand is the one who can write you a check. And if you don't understand what that product means to him, you have failed. Nothing in your marketing plan will make sense. All the advertising, great distribution, spectacular promotions, everything will fail because you don't know what it is you sell.

Key tips:

1. Understand what your product really is, based on the *customer's* values

2. Determine what makes your product distinct from competition—beyond functionality

3. Understand that "something else."

In summary:

Your customer needs your product to achieve their goals. They only want your product in relationship to those goals. Their goals change with time. If you understand the change—and meet it, the customer will stay with you. Otherwise, they'll be your competitor's customer.

What is distribution?

Distribution? A whole chapter on distribution?

Sure. We all think we know all about distribution but this is one of the more difficult areas to manage in marketing. Why? Because so many marketers—and others—don't really appreciate all that it is.

What's so hard about this? Distribution, at least according to marketing textbooks is simple. Distributors buy large quantities and sell in small quantities, thus adding value. They also provide "place" or a convenient place for the purchaser to buy, another added value and how the "D" in distribution became a "P" as in place so we have the 4Ps instead of the 3Ps and a D.

Then those MBA classes went on to teach the relative merits of "push" versus "pull" marketing.

What nonsense.

Push/pull had to be something invented by a professor who hadn't spent much time in the market. There really is no such thing as push marketing anymore than there is pushing toothpaste into a tube. As we'll explore later, "push" marketing is simply delegating your marketing to distribution—and delegating your profits at the same time.

The problem with the concept is symptomatic with much of the problems marketers have with distribution. They are looking at it from their perspective. This is like trying to examine the moon looking through the wrong end of the telescope. It's amazing how prevalent this is.

Every year at the Hardware Show the big box retailers hold manufacturer presentations. The manufacturers come crawling on their knees, bowing to the cardinal points of the compass as they worship before the god of the big box.

"Please carry our products. Please let us have more shelf space. We'll do anything. How about a larger promotional allowance? How about more co-op funds? Perhaps a bigger margin? We have better merchandising, these hard-hitting displays, better point-of-sale signage. We're into category management. Oh please. Oh please."

We're push marketing.

Yeech. What this sounds like to me is the pleading of manufacturers that fail to understand marketing so they "delegate" it to distribution.

Good luck.

And this is not just in the hardware category. Every category where distribution has been overrun by big box—electronics, furniture, toys, and, of course, the 80,000 pound gorilla, Wal-

Mart—the scene is pretty much the same. Except for a few manufacturers who get it.

Oh, but these distributors are my loyal customers. I've known them for years. We play golf together. (Who pays the greens fees? Why?) Are you really so naïve as to think that your distributor buddies will sacrifice their business to help you make a bigger profit?

Say it ain't so.

The Promise and Threat of Distribution

For many manufacturers, the promise of distribution is simple. Distributors have the customers. Our manufacturer wants to be carried by the strongest distributors because they have the most customers. Then they want to be carried by all the distributors.

While this may be critical to the start-up company with no customers, to the rest of you it's potential death.

Or at least an expensive way to live.

You have left your marketing to your distributors.

They control your business. They tell how much and what to make. They tell you what they'll pay. And a few months from now they may change their minds.

In business school, one of the more famous cases in business law concerned a company called Yardbird. They made lawn mowers. Then they landed Sears as a customer. And Sears took more and more of their production until Yardbird had only one customer, Sears. Then Sears put the squeeze on them, and eventually cancelled their orders. The company went out of business.

This should have been a marketing case, a prime example of what happens if you seem to think that distributors are your customers. They aren't. They're distributors. And they're in business to make money. And that might mean making money that you feel should be yours.

If you're to market successfully through distribution, you need to turn that telescope around. You have to look at your business through the eyes of the distributor. Then you need to step even further away and look at both the distributor's business and yours through the eyes of the end user, the consumer.

The Real Business of Distribution

Should you think that you are in a challenging business, walk a few miles in the shoes of your distributors. Consider this:

Your distributor has no control over the products he handles other than to handle them or not. He cannot change the product, only perhaps the packaging. He takes it pretty much as it comes. His competitors down the street handle the same products—unless you are in one of the few markets that feature exclusive distributors.

In other words, from your distributor's point of view he sells a commodity. His customer can purchase it from several sources.

The box of Tide your favorite grocery handles is no different than the box of Tide handled by the other grocery farther on down the street. The Timken bearing handled by the distributor you're dealing with now is no different that the Timken bearing handled by the other distributor across town.

For the grocer, his box of Tide is a commodity. Same with the bearing. Same with distribution in general. The products are commodities—you, their customer, can purchase them from several sources—the only difference is price—perhaps.

Why should you, the customer, come to a particular distributor? Why show him loyalty? What are the distributor's alternatives?

He can sell on price. If he rigorously pursues a low cost operation, he might survive.

He can attempt to distinguish himself through the total assortment of products he carries. He can become a supermarket for your product category. A "one stop shop."

He can attempt to distinguish himself on service. Delivery. Installation. Repair. Training.

He can attempt to differentiate himself through developing an intimate knowledge of his customers.

Most distributors try a combination of all. But they tend to develop distinctiveness.

Consider Home Depot and the small hardware store. Home Depot seems to have it all. But, in fact, their quality levels are generally middle-of-the-road. They usually don't carry the very high-end or specialty products as they don't turn over enough. And they do little in special order. The small store may not carry all the high-end product either but they will get it for you in less than a week.

Home Depot tries hard to offer advice and training. The small store often goes farther to provide the specific knowledge you need.

Both these stores see themselves as competitive but they are serving different customers with very different needs. And they can both survive and prosper.

Here are the challenges each face now that they both have figured out the basics to survive.

The most important point to remember is that both have a commitment to their employees and particularly their stockholders to grow. And if they're public, they most likely have promised to grow faster than the market in general. The tyranny of Wall Street.

The big box store built its franchise on lower price with a phenomenal selection of merchandise. It initially was the cheapest place to buy. If you are to exist over time as the biggest discounter, you have to develop fantastic discipline. You have to squeeze every penny out of your costs, your supply chain/ logistics cost and the costs of your suppliers. And you have to do this year after year. There is always a new contender willing to take your place.

Low cost is not usually a matter of innovation. There is little intellectual property to protect with patents and trademarks. You just have to be sure you're disciplined about your costs throughout the value chain day after day, year after year.

In the back of the mind of every one of Sam Walton's kids, they remember that there were discounters before Sam. Venture, K-Mart to name two. And they lost their discipline. Wal-Mart tried harder, was smarter.

Before Home Depot and Lowes there was Hechingers and Builder's Square. Before Best Buy and Circuit City there was Crazy Eddie's

The low price leader is a very difficult position to maintain.

On the other hand, our small hardware store has survived the Home Depot onslaught through superior service and handling products at the higher end of the spectrum. If you think managing low cost is a challenge, the consistent management of high-touch, high service is just as difficult, if not more so. Hiring, training and motivating employees is critical. And one bad employee, just one good employee having a bad day can lose customers who don't come back. When you depend on a smaller number of customers to return again and again, losing one is a much bigger problem than Home Depot has when they lose a customer.

The distributor who is building his business based on service faces the critical issue of marketing every day with every transaction:

> **The goal of your marketing is to create and nurture customer relationships.**

And consider that distribution is about as pure a marketing business as you can get.

Generally the smaller the distributor and the higher their price level, the more critical is their service.

That's what makes a boutique a boutique. And for the smaller store, managing the high level of service is not too difficult. The owner is usually on premise most of the time. The staff is small. The owner has a firm commitment to their style of service. And the owners and their small staff make a concerted effort to learn the preferences of their customers.

Now consider Neiman Marcus or Bloomingdale's. They have spent millions developing computer systems—and the attendant training—to help them build client relationships. To form customer relationships, learn and remember preferences, respond to the unique tastes of each of their customers. This is terrifically difficult for a firm the size of a large department store. Yet, they do it.

There is little you buy at Neiman Marcus that you can pay *more* for somewhere else. And much of what you buy you can purchase for less if you shop around. But you won't find anyone more willing to go out of their way to make sure you're pleased—delighted—with your purchase. And if you're not, they'll turn heaven and earth to make it right.

Yes, you might find similar quality for less but you won't get that kind of service along with it.

To sum up here:

> The high-end distributor is dedicated to building customer relationships.
> The discounter is working 24/7 to be the lowest of the low. There are all kinds in between trying to own a special niche.

And they are all working damn hard. Gaining and keeping customers is hard work.

So Along Comes You

Now you come along with your product and you expect these distributors to just let you take advantage of their market position, their customer relationships to build your business.

Think again. What are you going to do for them?

How are they to know your product will sell to their customer? That their customers will be satisfied over the life of the product? They do know it will take up space—and inventory dollars—that could be used for product that they know will sell.

Another Perspective

Look at it this way:

> Take the price the end customer pays for your product

The Failure of Marketing

Subtract your fully burdened product cost

Subtract the costs experienced by the distributor

The result is the profit you and the distributor share

So who gets the most? Who determines who gets how much?

First let's recognize that both you and the distributor need to have a profit. If you don't, you'll stop making the product; if the distributor doesn't, he won't carry the product. In each case there is eventually no profit for either of you. But in between these two extremes there is plenty of room for movement.

Consider the grocery trade. Thirty years ago, the manufacturers had the greater control. Their brand names really had power. They made considerably more than the grocer. But over the next twenty years, the balance shifted dramatically. Now the grocers are extracting profits from the manufacturers through a variety of fees and surcharges for slotting, promotions, and displays. In the sixties this was unheard of.

Why the shift? The balance of power resides in one simple concept:

Who owns the customer relationship?

Back in the 1960's, if you as a grocer were out of Minute Maid orange juice, your customers would head to another store to purchase it. And perhaps purchase other items, maybe even shifting their loyalty to the new store. Now, if you're out of it, they'll purchase Tropicana or your house brand even though they prefer the other brand.

What's happened is simple. The relationship the customer had with the brand has decreased while the relationship they have with the store has increased—and become the greater of the two. The store now calls the shots.

107

If you don't own the customer relationship, you are treading on thin ice.

What will happen if the distributor decides to cancel you?

What will you do when the distributor feels you should pay for their advertising? Or their stocking? Or their delivery? Or their sales efforts? The consumer packaged goods manufacturers have been asking themselves this for the past three decades. The answers haven't been to their liking.

The Critical Issue

Who will have the stronger customer relationship, you or your distributor? What's it going to be? You or the distributor?

Distributors out in the market do all kinds of things to build and maintain customer relationships. For example:

> Ingersoll-Rand distributors provide extensive installation, service and repair, spare parts, and ancillary equipment to customers. Some even offer rental programs. They'll come into a customer and offer a total package from system design to equipment, installation and maintenance.

> Whole Foods has large sections with precooked food in a cafeteria setting, an extensive deli section, and entrees to take home and heat. It's a common trend in the grocery business to offer much of what a take-out restaurant offers.

> Steel service centers have moved far beyond purchasing steel in bulk and selling smaller amounts to customers. They'll provide inventory management, cutting and forming, parts fabrication, and some are even into finishing operations.

Grainger has grown from simply being the largest distributor to industry to offering a wide variety of product specific services. Want to purchase lighting? Grainger will provide an installer. Need safety equipment? Grainger can sell you the equipment or take it farther with safety consultants. They don't just sell equipment; they solve problems.

And the list just goes on forever:

BP has a huge business with convenience stores at their gas stations. They have even experimented with a significant change in emphasis where their stations look more like convenience stores selling gas.

Your grocery store offers cooking classes. And so does your local kitchen store. There have never been more places to learn how to cook.

The cosmetics departments in department stores will help you with your makeup, from a complete makeover to facials.

Home Depot has a regularly scheduled and professional staffed group conducting "how to" classes at their stores.

Costco has absolutely the best lunch deal in their stores. And, of course, department stores have had restaurants from lunch counters to full-service restaurants for years. When Macy's took over Marshall Field & Co. a major concern in Chicago was what would happen to the Walnut Room on the seventh floor. It stayed.

Empire Carpet—call today, carpet tomorrow—now does wood floors, blinds and window treatments, siding and gutters, windows, and now bathroom refinishing.

Some have even gone so far they aren't called distributors any more—they're VARs—value-added resellers, essentially systems integrators. They reached their zenith in the market for computer systems, helping customers define their needs, then providing a custom-tailored solution of components to best meet that need. The customer has little knowledge of the component brands other than the name staring back from the monitor and the logo of the operating system at start-up.

So what's going on here? Aren't distributors happy with their assigned role of place? Do they want to become manufacturers? No, the smart ones have learned a cool marketing principle:

If you provide greater value to the customer, you can build a stronger relationship (and develop additional lines of income).

And because they're so close to the customers, dealing with them every day, they find out very quickly what the customer values and how they can respond.

What are you doing to learn about your customer—not the distributor—but the one who uses your product?

How to tell who gets how much margin

Consider a relatively simple situation: the purchase of branded product in a supermarket—Charmin Tissue, for example. The store is out of stock. What are you going to do? For the shopper you need to consider the total value proposition:

- How important is the uniqueness of the product compared to the entire shopping experience?

110

- Are there so many other things at that store that you'll stay and purchase another brand?
- Or is the product so good you'll go elsewhere for everything?
- Or will you purchase some things at your first store and some more at the next store?
- How many stores will you go visit to find the Charmin?
- Is Charmin that much different than a competitive brand—Northern, for example?
- Is there another store conveniently located?
- Is there parking?
- Do you have the time?
- Will they take your check?
- Are there other products you also need to purchase somewhere else?
- Are there loyalty points at this store?
- Are the prices comparable at the alternative stores?

These are just a few of the questions going through the mind of the shopper. The totality of the answers is directly proportional to the amount of the margin you'll share with the distributor.

In other words, you need to know the relative importance of the factors that make up the customer's value proposition.

In the above simple case, if the customer values the softness of the product over the effort to go to another store, Charmin wins and gets the big bucks.

Now let's consider something much more complicated. Wall-to-wall carpet. Your carpet that was in your home when you moved in is now showing signs of wear. So off you go to the carpet store. In the earlier example, the customer knew exactly what she wanted—Charmin. Now you only know what type of carpet you want—green, plush carpet. Should you have polyester, nylon or wool? How thick? What kind of stain-resistance? What brand?

Your primary source of information is the carpet sales person.

What's his primary interest? Seeing you get the best carpet for your needs? Seeing that he gets the spiff from one of the manufacturers? Seeing that he gets points for moving a brand their buyers over-purchased? Selling you the most expensive carpet in the store thus improving his productivity numbers—and bonus?

You will never know. But I do know this: you will not be going to another store because you can't find the brand you want. If you do go, it will be to hear what another retailer has to offer. Your choice is more about which retailer you trust than what carpet you want.

And the retailer is making more than the carpet manufacturer.

Back to the first example, P&G spends millions on market research and millions more on product research to make sure you prefer Charmin. And while Charmin alone may not cause you to change retailer, a combination of Charmin, Tide, Bounce, Folgers, Puffs and maybe a few other brands and you're off to a new store. That's why very few retailers are ever out of any P&G brand. P&G is so very focused on building and maintaining a relationship with their consumers and this pays off in their dealings with retailers.

But He's Your Friend

The distributor of yours, he is your friend, right? Well, personally, he might be your friend. But from the point of view of your business he's the distributor. Keep in mind that he has competition also. He has to build and maintain customer relationships. He has to out-market his competition. He has to build his margins so he can afford to keep the competitive pressure on.

When your distributor friend is staring at a tough competitive situation, eyeball-to-eyeball, who do you think is going to get the benefit of the doubt? You? Or him?

When you haven't established a relationship with your consumer, your distributor knows he has the upper hand. He may appreciate that you need to make a profit, but he also knows that he can squeeze your profit to the bone. Remember, this is business.

Look at this from the distributor's point of view. He has worked hard to build his customer base and you come along and want him to distribute your product to that clientele. Why should he do that? These are his customers. He has worked hard to build up a relationship. And now you expect him to just let you take advantage of that relationship?

Is he supposed to take your product in and introduce it to these customers?

What if the product doesn't live up to the customer's expectations? Will he have to pay the price for that?

Your distributor is supposed to stock your product, provide service for your product, and provide sales support for your product—to his customer base—all for the standard distributor margin.

What marketing do you do?

In other words, this close distributor friend of yours is to accept all of the marketing responsibilities, and all of the marketing risks, while you accept a lion's share of the profits.

No.

The way this usually works is that your distributor friend takes on your product with minimal support, consistent with other products in your category. And when one of your competitors comes along and offers a better deal your distribution channel is gone.

Consider this real situation:

The company has sold its products through the hardware channel since it was founded. A member of AHAM. Close to the major chains. And thirty years ago they dealt with buying groups, wholesalers, Ace and True Value. They had hundreds of accounts.

They did no consumer advertising or promotion. Consumer marketing was the job of the retailer—at least in their minds. They made a good product, shipped on time and it sold at a reasonable price. Everyone happy? Not quite.

There is always competition. And they worked hard to keep up, new products, improved products, line extensions, fighting brands.

But in general, the risk was minimal. If one store dropped their product they would hardly notice. They didn't like it but it was far from life-threatening.

But over the last twenty years, distribution has changed dramatically. The Big Box is in. The independent is gone. Distribution isn't friendly anymore.

They want deals. Stocking deals, coop deals, display deals and a total product program. And if you also intend to sell through their competitors, well don't bother coming in.

You don't push your product through this type of distribution without paying a hearty cost.

And when someone comes along with a better offer, a better product or a product the consumer prefers—you're gone. In a flash. It happened to them at one account and they lost 30% of their sales in a heartbeat.

Distribution has changed. It is an extraordinarily competitive business and no matter what industry you're in—grocery, steel, hardware, fashion, plastics—distribution does not come cheap.

But still, today, too many manufacturers continue to make the great distribution marketing mistake:

They delegate their marketing to distribution.

But the distributor can be your partner.

Perhaps this has seemed a little harsh, cold blooded, at this point. But you have to realize, when you follow the dollars, you and your distributors compete with each other.

As long as you both view your relationship as a zero sum game.

It doesn't have to be. It just takes a simple change in attitude.

For example,

> Ingersoll-Rand compressor marketing people maintain a dialogue with their end users. The conversation is a constant one with three participants: the I-R marketing management, the distributor and the end user. The subject is always the same—how can we provide the end user with more value. What can the distributor do? How can I-R help the distributor do it? What should I-R be responsible for? What should their distributor handle?

A simple example—packaged goods with Procter & Gamble. As noted earlier they go out of their way to maintain a relationship with their customer. They do the same with their distribution. They created and continue to develop their "store of the future", an idea lab of packaged goods retailing. Concepts developed here continually make their way into their distributors. They have taken great steps to facilitate the introduction of scanners and other methods to track sales and inventory along with customer behavior. They see themselves as a partner with the grocery trade and realize that their success depends on the success of their distribution.

Examples abound here:

The Saturn automobile project was based not only on a new car concept but on a new way of managing the car dealer/customer relationship.

All-Clad cookware helps their dealers with extensive training and in-store assistance.

Several firms have developed a limited number of prototype stores to serve as models in a market—Apple, Nike and Cole Hahn, Levi's, Garmin, Hershey's, Sony. The stores provide service that the retail channel can't afford, provide a total look at their products and set a price ceiling that distribution can appreciate.

What these examples all have in common is that both the manufacturer and the distributor have a clear understanding of the consumer's purchase decision. They understand the buyer's values and needs and have decided amongst themselves who is the most capable of fulfilling them. The result of this cooperation and mutual understanding is a growth in consumer satisfaction, which leads to increasing sales for both the distributor and the manufacturer along with a deeper and more satisfactory relationship.

These partnerships between manufacturer, distribution and customer work to the advantage of all. The consumer gets a broader and deeper value proposition, the manufacturer stays close to the consumer and can anticipate new needs and maximize the value of the product while the distributor can do what he does best, tailor service to meet the unique needs of the consumer.

But you only have a partnership when the manufacturer realizes it has a major responsibility to build and maintain a relationship with the consumer. It's their product. They are the only ones in control of it and its basic value proposition.

It only works if they avoid the basic mistake of distribution . . . .

The Great Distribution Marketing Mistake

The distributor is not your customer. He is only the distributor. Your customer, the one paying for all your salaries, your materials, your cost of capital is the end user. If you ignore the end user, distribution will eat your lunch—as well they should.

You must be a partner with distribution in building the relationship with the end user.

Distribution versus Value Chains

In the past fifteen years distribution and logistics have become hot topics. With the logistical innovation of Dell and UPS, with the emphasis on logistics and the attendant costs by Wal-Mart, logistics has reached a prominence resulting in a remarkable

117

attention, even a whole category of magazines focused entirely on the supply chain.

Correspondingly, there has been a renewed emphasis on the value chain, which, by the way, has little to do with logistics. The understanding of value chain is particularly important to manufacturers supplying parts and components that eventually find their way to OEMs.

For example, iron ore is mined by a company in northern Minnesota and sold to a steel company in Cleveland. That company turns it into steel ingots which are then sold to a subsidiary company that turns it into steel rod. The rod is purchased by a company making spark plugs which are sold to automotive OEMs, installed in cars, sold to dealers who, in turn, sell to you. That's the path of the ore from mine to you, each player in the chain adding value.

A value chain looks at what value each of the producers creates in that path and who benefits from that value. For example, the mining company ships ore particularly high in iron. They charge more for it and they receive the value. The steel maker pays more for it because it yields more steel and has less waste to discard.

However, let's say the steel formulation that the manufacturer makes is particularly suited for turning into spark plugs which will be more reliable in the car, producing better gas mileage. While every member of the value chain—steel maker, rod maker, plug maker, auto maker, and dealer— benefits from having a product more tailored to their own marketing needs, you, as the buyer of the car are the final beneficiary.

You get better gas mileage and you are willing to pay a bit more for the car because of that. You will also purchase the same plugs when it's time to replace them, even though the store charges more for them.

You don't really benefit from the efficiency of the ore producer but you do benefit from the metallurgical skills of the steel maker.

Why is this important to understand? Because while you may pay more, it won't go to the steelmaker unless you connect your benefit, higher gas mileage, to the steel maker rather than the plug manufacturer.

Consider Intel. Intel Inside.

They are not spending millions on advertising for the sake of their ego. They realize that the true beneficiary of their ingenuity is you. You are able to run more complex programs, to run them faster, to have a computer that will be more reliable and last longer because of their engineering prowess in designing CPU chips.

And they want to make sure you know that. Then you'll be willing to pay more for a computer that has their chip inside. And then they can charge more to the computer OEM, knowing that he'll make more also.

On one hand, you could consider the OEM a chip distributor, or possibly a value-added reseller. But as much as the computer OEM talks about customizing their product, they are primarily manufacturers with set product lines. They don't see themselves as either distributors or VARs.

Here's another example. Back in the early 1990's Amoco Chemicals (now Flint Hills Resources) was manufacturing Purified Isophthalic Acid (PIA). One of the uses of the product was in formulating the polyester resin used in fiberglass. And a major use of the resin was in making recreational boats.

A major problem with a fiberglass boat at that time was that if it was moored in salt water and stayed in the water too long, the fiberglass would develop blisters. These had to be repaired or eventually the resin would fail.

Amoco developed a new polyester resin formulation using PIA that dramatically reduced the tendency of the resin to blister.

They took the formulation to their customer, the resin manufacturers, but they had no interest. The boat business was extremely cost competitive and they did not feel they could pass on the higher cost of the resin to their customer, the boat builder.

So Amoco went to the boat builder. He said the same thing. Too costly and no chance to pass on the cost to the boat dealer.

So on to the dealer, where they heard pretty much the same thing, no chance to pass the cost on to the boat buyer.

Now when the boat blisters, none of these people—the resin manufacturer, the boat builder, the dealer—had to deal with it. Not their problem. The boat owner had to fix the blisters at his own cost, taking the boat out of the water at a yard and either paying the yard or doing it himself. Costly. Time consuming. And a royal pain.

Amoco took the final step and talked with the boat owner. They would be delighted to pay much, much more if the resin wouldn't blister. So Amoco promoted to the owners that they needed to ask for resins formulated with Amoco PIA when they went to purchase their next boat.

Within two years, every major boat builder had signs on their boats at the Miami Boat Show that they used PIA-based resins. Amoco sold a lot of PIA and made a lot of money.

One last example that I mentioned earlier. DuPont figured out how to coat nylon fiber with Teflon, making it stain resistant. They licensed their process to their nylon customers who made yarn for carpet, and then sold their yarn to the carpet manufacturer who in turn sold to the dealer who sells to you.

At that time, the dealer controlled carpet marketing. No manufacturers had enough brand presence to impact the market. It had not always been that way. Prior to the 1950s the carpet manufacturers had built strong brands—Karastan, Bigelow and others. But with the growth of the suburbs and the tremendous demand for wall-to-wall carpet, the manufacturers had no reason, they thought, to continue to support their brand. Why advertise when you're selling all your factory can produce?

They learned.

When demand returned to a more normal level, the manufacturers were essentially unknown and the dealer was the prime source of information for the consumer. And he did what was best for the dealer. The carpet producer was manufacturing a commodity. The dealer provided the value. And took the majority of the margin. Most of the carpet manufacturers prior to the fifties are gone. The dealers took their profits and only the most cost efficient survived.

Until DuPont came along. DuPont spent heavily on introducing Stainmaster to the home owner. And the carpet dealer ran into a challenge. Customers were walking into the store and asking for Stainmaster. And if it wasn't there, they went elsewhere—elsewhere being a competitive retailer. So the dealer demanded Stainmaster from the manufacturer, and DuPont made plenty of money.

That's from understanding the value chain. It's not exactly distribution. But one principle is absolutely clear in both cases:

> Who controls the relationship with the end user makes the money.

Chapter 8

Third P—Promotion

Nothing in marketing is quite as exciting for the young ad manager, product manager, marketing manager and agency person as going on that first commercial shoot. Wow, this is the big leagues.

I know. I was there.

Early '70s. Off to L.A. with an expense account almost as large as my salary. We flew first class, stayed at a great hotel in Westwood, rented several Mercedes. The marketing manager and I had spent several weeks before the shoot scoping out what was new in the restaurant scene. This client was covering all expenses and considered a commercial shoot part of a paid vacation.

Prior to the shoot, I was having a difficult time accepting that the average cost of a commercial was over $100,000. But when I got on the location, all became clear.

Who were all these people?

The director and his staff, the location scouts, the casting staff, the lighting crew, the sound crew, the make-up and hairdressing staff, the production assistants running around finding props, the camera crew, carpenters, drivers, and a few cops (which make you really feel important). And then, of course, are the actors perhaps with agent/friend/family in tow. And we, well, the client, was paying for all this. Every single person. Including me.

But that was L.A. and in the '70s. 'Tis changed. Now the shoots are all over the place, Toronto, Vancouver, Orlando, Albuquerque, Dallas, you name it. Supposedly to get around the unions and some crazy work rules. But the cost is still through the roof. It's now somewhere around $400,000 for the average commercial. Consider this: at that rate for 30 seconds of finished film, a 2 hour movie would cost about $96,000,000. No name actors, directors, writers, no blowing up buildings, no intentional car crashes, just a plain average commercial.

But production is only the start.

Oh, you say, you want to put this little commercial on TV? Well, don't forget the talent fees. Their session fee covers the first few weeks. But if you want to run it some more, you have to pay additional usage fees. If you don't want to run it for a while but want to run it later, well, there are holding fees to pay when you're not running it. These talent fees all add up to a tidy little sum.

And then there's the media. TV is not cheap. You can get into the hundreds of millions very fast. Let's just leave it at that.

TV is the "Big Kahuna" of promotion and promotion is the fun part of marketing, putting together advertising and seeing it on television, in magazines, or on the web, creating events and tradeshow extravaganzas, meeting with editors; promotion is dramatic and exciting and fun.

Promotion, however, is a misnomer created to fit into the "4P's". A much better, more descriptive name is marketing communications. As marketing communications, it covers an extremely broad array of activities including:

    Television advertising
    Magazine advertising
    Radio advertising
    Newspaper advertising
    Direct mail
    Outdoor boards
    Transit boards
    Internet sites
    Website advertising
    Search advertising
    E-mail advertising
    Blogging
    Message boards
    Tradeshows
    User meetings
    Events
    Market publicity
    Product publicity
    Product placements
    Word-of-mouth stimulation
    Speaking tours
    Packaging
    Point-of-sale
    Product displays

And whatever else the marketing communications department, media and marketing services agencies can create.

This is an enormous array of activities. But they all have one thing in common; they are directed at influencing the behavior of customers and prospects.

And marketing communication often commands a dizzying budget.

As discussed in the last chapter, if you are to have any control over distribution, you have to generate interest and preference from the consumer. To do that, you must communicate with your market.

While marketing communications attracts more attention in marketing than any other subject, it also is subject to more failures. Here are the big ones—an even dozen.

Failure #1: Who Is Your Market?

I can understand how a commercial on a TV show in prime time will not necessarily be directed at me. Even easier, I can understand why a show in daytime appeals to women. However, when I look at the ten or so pieces of mail I receive every day, personally addressed to me that are totally inappropriate I wonder. The direct mail industry is supposed to be so good at tightly defining a market.

In the past week I have received mail offering car insurance—I don't own a car; a promotion for a country music festival—not my thing; membership in an all-woman's spa—I'm male; and at least ten credit card offerings—I already have more than I use and don't carry balances.

All these dead trees from people who are claiming to be the experts in targeting.

The Failure of Marketing

Tightly defining the audience for your marketing communications is the greatest challenge you face—and the first challenge you face.

If your target is wrong you have totally failed. If your target is partially off, you have partially failed. A communication directed to someone who is not in the market is a total waste.

Since the beginning of mass media, loosely defined targets have been accepted as necessary waste when reaching your valuable desired target. It reduces to a simple cost equation. The reach is so cheap that accepting the waste is more efficient than paying for a more tightly targeted audience.

But targeting in mass media is based on a few demographics and rather crude measures at that.

But we now have an incredible selection of tightly targeted mailing lists, narrowly focused magazines—who will also sell their circulation lists, plus an ever expanding selection of internet sites with extremely tight targets. Precise, laser-like targeting with less waste is becoming easier and easier.

But . . .

This assumes you know who your customer is—who your prospect is.

Are you guessing, or do you really know? Are you actually measuring, monitoring, researching who your customer is?

Do you know their demographics?

Do you know how your customers differ from your competitors?

If I describe a customer to you, will you be able to tell me whether he's your customer or your competitors?

If you're guessing at all of this, then don't go any further. Until you solve this problem any marketing communications will be a waste.

A total failure.

Failure #2: Will any road get you there?

Setting the right objectives for marketing communications activities is the next fundamental challenge. Without setting appropriate objectives, the possibility of having excellent marketing communications is slim, in fact, a matter of chance. But consider this. The general goal of marketing itself is to create and nurture customer relationships. Marketing communications, as a part of marketing, must then have objectives that support this marketing objective.

At the same time objectives must meet the two standards of basic good objectives, that is:

1. They need to be measurable.

2. They need to be specific.

But too often the objectives are so fuzzy as to be meaningless. How will you get good marketing communications when objectives are set as:

> Create an ad
> Develop a mailing program to *(your target here)*.
> Make our website better than competition's
> Introduce our new product

These are not objectives, just names of activities. Intent. The same intent every marketer has.

Objectives should specify an endpoint, some place you wish to reach appropriate to communication. And in moving towards that end point the objective should be consistent with the overall marketing objectives that will result in creating and nurturing customer relationships.

They should also imply measurement. The objective, "to build awareness of—," is not a good objective. It needs a specific numerical goal such as increasing awareness by 25%. This, of course, means that you need to know how much awareness you have,. which means you have to conduct some market research.

Many marketing communications practitioners argue that the objective for marketing communications should be awareness of some body of knowledge, like awareness of a brand. This is setting a low bar and is often just plain lazy.

"We need to build awareness of the company."

Don't we all?

Easily accomplished. Consider the awareness of Tylenol after their adulteration problem. Or the awareness of Enron. Martha Stewart.

Underneath the awareness goal is the loose assumption that the awareness should be positive. So what is positive?

What is necessary is that there be comprehension among the audience. That should be the general framework of the objective.

Understanding.

Belief.

But of what? That takes us into the next failure.

Failure #3: What will move the needle?

As mentioned earlier, back in the late 50s or early 60s marketers had a brilliant flash of insight: products had features and benefits, and benefits were different than features.

As a refresher, features are a property of the product such as being made of steel. A benefit is something valued by the owner of the product, such as durability which is derived from the product being made of steel. And you'll notice the implied relationship; benefits are dependent upon features.

Well, this seems pretty easy and straightforward. Benefits are the value each of us place on features. And this would be pretty easy except that each of us have slightly different values. If we didn't, we'd all be living in houses that look identical, driving identical cars, wearing identical clothes, and all trying to get into the same schools, restaurants, stores, movie theaters—to watch the same movie, standing in a very long line.

Obviously, we don't all have the same values and as a result we value benefits differently. A feature that you may value highly may have little value to your neighbor and maybe is negative for me. A simple example: you may love your SUV while your neighbor may prefer small, nimble sports cars, and because I live in the city, owning a big vehicle like that causes nothing but parking headaches. Same vehicle, different values, different benefit levels.

So what does this have to do with marketing communications? Simply this. You have to understand what your market values, what it sees as a benefit, prior to setting your objective. How many commercials have you seen where you know you're in the target audience and yet you take nothing away from it? They offered nothing you valued.

Have you ever done that?

The failure here is twofold. Either the marketing communications is asserting a benefit where none are valued by the market, or the communications are highlighting a feature that has no obvious benefit. So what if the product is made from steel? What's that supposed to mean to me?

Here's why this is critical to your marketing communications. If you are to move the needle, to inspire your market to change their behavior and begin a relationship with you rather than your competition, you have to promise them something they value. And that value or the amount of that value has to be unique to you.

Too many companies make promises that seem grand—to them. But to the market—no value. A waste of money. A failure.

Now this is where it gets difficult. What people say they value and what, in fact, they actually value are generally entirely different. Imagine that!

This leads us to market research challenges and failures, several chapters away.

Suffice it to say at this point, asking the designer or engineer, asking the sales force, asking anyone other than the market what the market values can cost you loads of money in wasted advertising. It also won't help your career to have so big and visible a failure.

Don't guess. Find out.

Failure #4: Communicate

Now that you know what will move the market, a marketing decision, you're faced with an even more difficult decision, a huge opportunity for failure: how to say it.

Well, just say it. Clear, concise language. Right?

Wrong.

Clear, concise language is for instruction manuals and the help menu. They have a simple goal—to explain to people who are seeking information. Direction.

You need to do much more. "Communicate" means that the other person understands and internalizes what you said and mean.

And you are trying to persuade.

You need to stand out from the 3000+ commercial messages each of us sees a day. Messages we are not looking for. You need to persuade us to believe what you are saying. You need to create impact for your message so we remember.

These are the key words for communication—stand out, persuade, remember. And this all has to be done with style consistent with your product, service, company and promise.

And respect for your audience.

If you hear an announcer screaming about how good he is, well, you know he's working for a car dealer. And you dismiss the message. They fail.

How do you attract attention, attract interest? You need to be able to craft words your audience wants to hear. And we want to hear about ourselves, our problems, our opportunities and how you might be able to help us.

Perhaps you need to show us, demonstrate.

Perhaps you need to empathize, show us how you understand.

There are, perhaps, many ways more. A theatre professor back in college made us say "no" forty different ways.

Can you find ten different ways to present your message to your audience? Clearly, respectfully? Which one will capture their attention best? Least/ Most persuasively? Most memorably?

No one said this was easy. How much is this worth to you? Maybe you should hire experts.

Failure #5: Hollow words

"Quality. The market does not understand our quality."

Ever said that? Ever heard that? What is it supposed to mean? Most of the time, I've heard it said when someone's lost an order to a lower price. But, what is quality?

(Note: If you want to get into a philosophical discussion on quality, we are not going to do it here. But I would suggest you start with the book, *Zen and the Art of Motorcycle Maintenance*, by Robert Pirsig (1974). It's a fun read.)

"Quality" is a hollow claim. It's what you claim when your have no idea what to claim. Everybody claims "quality." No one claims, "Lousy quality."

"We make our product with quality materials." No, actually, we make them out of crap materials.

Come on, think a little. Surely you can do better than "quality."

The word has no meaning to the customer. But I still see it in ads, in brochures, on packages. What it signifies is that the writer was lazy and didn't care about me, the customer.

Luxury. Downtown Chicago has been going through a residential renaissance. My old dentist's office is now somebody's condo. Office buildings, old factory buildings, warehouses, all are seeing renewed life as condo buildings.

And then come the developers of new buildings. What do they have to sell?

Luxury Apartments. Luxury Condominiums. Always, luxury.

Can't they think of a different word? It would only have meaning if more of the properties offered dark, dingy, cold, cramped apartments. But then what would they claim on their signs? Quality?

These words have no meaning because with their overuse they have become disconnected from their referent. Or they've been used to attract buyers, who upon inspection of the product, come to the opposite conclusion.

Here are a few more:

> Perfect
> Deluxe
> Fast
> Tastes great
> Special
> Value
> Limited

I love "limited." It's one of my favorites. I received an invitation a month ago to a seminar—attendance was limited. An email the day prior to the seminar urged quick action—attendance was limited. The next morning, you guessed it, it was still limited. This causes one to ask, "Limited to what?"

Obviously, "limited" by this group was just a ploy to urge action. What nonsense. But when your message is judged as nonsense that judgment tends to extend to you.

Yes, you.

These, and many other words, are overused and, now, without meaning. They are the mark of lazy marketing. Instead of finding out what's really important, what really needs to be said, the marketer is taking the lazy way and using words of no meaning.

He is a failure.

And by using these words he continues to perpetuate the poor reputation of marketing communications.

And you.

One last word needs some discussion: Free.

Since the first copywriter emerged from the primordial swamp, the word, "Free" has been considered, "The most powerful word."

This is **THE WORD.**

But, it may be in deathly danger. When something is offered as free, it better have some value. And it better be completely free.

A free offer of no value is going to kill the power of the word. Moreover, it will kill any credibility and respect you have in the market.

A good friend who is quite the do-it-yourselfer received a mailing from a store selling tools and shop supplies. The mailing featured a new workshop-style vacuum cleaner that had all sorts of special features. And, if you came in to view it over the next several weeks, you would receive a free 10-piece tool set free. Just for coming in for a demo.

So, he went.

And he saw the demo, even tried it out himself. And he thought it was not quite up to what he had in mind, thank you very much. And then he asked for his 10-piece tool set.

And they went in the back and came out with a small cardboard box. Opening it, he saw a little plastic "tool case" and inside it had ten tiny little tools. The entire tool case was about 3" long. The screwdriver was an inch long.

As he said, "Just their way of telling me to f—off."

The store is gone. The word "free" suffered another hit.

When you offer something for free and it turns out to be junk, you are just demonstrating your contempt for the customer. And they will get back at you.

Stop it.

This is an important word. Save it. And save your own self-respect.

Failure #6: Agency Relationships

Ad agencies, PR agencies, direct response, promotion, internet, website, evangelist marketing, RSS, email agencies—they are all created to do what you don't want to do, don't know how to do, or can't afford to do.

Actually, most of them claim to have skill sets critical to aid your marketing. But so many just don't know what they should be doing—don't understand marketing—and their clients don't know what to tell them.

The problem starts out with a failure by the client: clearly, accurately and realistically defining the marketing objectives and extending them to the marketing communications objectives (see Failures #1, #2 and #3).

How is the agency to know what to do? Divine inspiration? If you can't even define your own objectives why expect the agency to meet them?

"Oh, but we selected them because they demonstrated such comprehensive knowledge of our market."

While this is often nice to have, it has little bearing on whether the agency is any good. Oh, the agency knows the largest dealers; they know your largest customer. So what? If they know them better than you, you should be ashamed.

Seriously ashamed.

The first task common to all communications is determining what to communicate. This is a marketing function. Is your agency supposed to do this? You're outsourcing your marketing. This is a core decision that the CMO should make. It's his responsibility. That's why he has the title, "Chief Marketing Officer."

He should have the essential message tattooed to the inside of his eyelid. He should know this in his sleep. But all too often, "Let's ask the agency."

Why should they know? They aren't in the market every day, like he should be. They might be if they handled all his competitors also but this is usually a violation of agency confidentiality.

They don't have a sales force in the market. They aren't getting calls from your dealers or your customers.

When you base your agency decision on their knowledge of the market you are admitting that their knowledge is better than yours. Doesn't this embarrass you?

It should.

First, the agency should be selected on their ability to take your message and craft it, present it in such that it will attract attention and be remembered. They are in charge of "how to say it". (see Failure #4.)

They must be experts at this. Rather than asking them to demonstrate their knowledge of your market, ask them to demonstrate how many ways they can present a specific message.

They should come up with at least 5, maybe 10.

Then ask them which one they think is the strongest and why.

Do any of the recommendations make the hair on the back of your neck stand up? Which one's make you feel a little uneasy?

Most good communications stretch the envelope a bit. Past your comfort zone. That's what makes them memorable.

Go on with whatever you're doing for another week. Then think back. Which of their efforts do you remember?

And once you've decided, leave it alone. You are not a writer. They are. Take their advice. Oh sure, perhaps a tweak or two. But only if you need to correct a factual or technical inaccuracy.

Early in my career I worked with a marketing manager who thought she was a writer. Our advertising agency's assignment was to prepare an ad directed at travel agents. We had an input meeting with the travel agent marketing manager where we got all the input that we needed.

We brought copy and layout back to the advertising manager. She proceeded to edit it and give it back to us for revisions. We considered the changes she made and suggested changes that we felt were stronger. She then made more changes. We suggested slightly different changes. She suggested even more changes.

We gave up. We retyped her copy, updated the layout and returned with them.

She modified that copy and layout. Once again we retyped her copy, updated the layout and returned with them.

She continued to do this at least 20 times. She was changing her own changes. We'd given up on recommendations. We had become exceptionally frustrated typists.

She, on the other hand, was costing her company a small fortune. When we approached the Executive Vice President for an increase in our monthly fee he wanted to know how we could justify that. I brought him all the copy and layouts that we had done and explained how much time they took. And time is money.

Eventually she was let go.

The next area of agency responsibility is media. This used to be a simple task. Then came direct mail. Then telemarketing, followed by direct response, then promotions and events, then email, websites, blogs, RSS, evangelists—and between the time I write this and when this eventually lands in your hands, a few more alternatives will be created.

Each of these media need specialized assistance. A message framed for a broad television audience won't cut it at an event. You need to adapt it.

Note:

> The "what to say" needs to stay the same. The "how to say it" is what changes.

You will maximize the impact of your marketing communications if you hire experts in these so specialized media. Just make sure they are experts.

The net of this: know what you're supposed to do—marketing. Know what they're supposed to do—communicating. They shouldn't have to do what you do.

Then let them do their best.

But that brings up the next possible failure—Integration.

Failure #7: Lack of Integration

First, this has nothing to do about race.

Looking through the archives, this was a fad in the mid-sixties, and then again in the mid-seventies, reemerged in the late-eighties and through most of the nineties. It should now be common practice.

But it's not.

It is a simple concept that should be easily and quickly understood.

But it's not.

It's called integrated marketing communications. It means that all communications work in a coordinated fashion to communicate with your customer and prospect audience. Essentially they all support a common strategic communications objective but are tailored for the idiosyncrasies of their medium.

For example, if your objective is to reinforce to your customer base that your products exemplify the properties of A, B, and C (in objective speak, "Maintain comprehension of promise A at the current 80% level . . . .) then your communications to your customers would all address these three properties. Envelope stuffers, promotional copy on bills, direct mail activities, ads. All focused on those three factors. And when the customer goes to your website the first information they'd see would reinforce those three properties.

If you go back to the earlier list of marketing communication activities, this means that you integrate the message so that each activity reinforces the message you're trying to communicate.

The Failure of Marketing

What is so hard about this?

Why should this be a recurring fad about every ten years?

Perhaps because:

- Product manager 1 needs to convince the market of message "S."

- Product manager 2 needs to convince the market of message "T."

- Product manager 3 needs to convince the market of message "U."

- The VP Sales wants to convince the market of "V," "W," and "X" today.

- Customer service forcefully recommends reminding the market of "Y."

- While the Director of Research is hung up on a study that would suggest at a confidence level of 95% the emphasis of property "Z."

Now, let's look at money. The VP marketing has a budget best described as modest. The rest have budgets which range from dinky to tiny.

However, when added all together, the total is respectable. But only if it is focused on one audience and one objective.

So, the VP Marketing does the only fair thing: *you* get a few ad pages, and *you* get a few also. *You*, over there, get a direct mail campaign while *you* get a few more web pages.

And because they each address a different interest, a different product, a different property, and none had enough exposure to be noticed, the entire effort is wasted.

Wasted. A failure.

Here is the ugly, little secret about marketing communications:

This is one weak tool for communication.

It has to do with something the media and your agency rarely tell you:

The market is not sitting out there politely, waiting breathlessly for your message. In fact, if it never comes, they won't be upset.

The average hour of television has twenty-two minutes of commercials, that's forty-four :30 spots. The average magazine is 60% advertising. Your mailbox has a ton or two of direct mail in it. Plus the product placements, the publicity-managed articles, the talk show appearances, the web sites, internet ads, search engine optimization and the telemarketing calls to the three remaining people who are not on the FTC's Do Not Call List. Then there are the outdoor boards, the bus ads, the TDI boards in the airports, email on your Blackberry. And the packaging, point of sale, even the ads on the back of the receipt.

Some poor dude, probably a grad student doing research for his doctorate, calculated that each of us sees about 3000 commercial messages a day.

How many of those three thousand messages you saw yesterday do you remember today? Any? Like I was saying . . .

This is a weak tool for communication.

So, the most common way to try and overcome the weakness is to repeat your message. And, the theory goes, if you repeat it often enough, forcefully enough, you can drive the message home.

But this costs money. Tons of it.

And you are frittering your budget amongst the competing needs of a fraternity of product managers, a sales manager with multiple directions, and a host of others. And you probably only have enough money for one simple, clear message.

Does your senior management have the discipline to mandate that there will only be one message? Or will the money have no impact by being spread around to dissipate into nothingness but another wasted opportunity?

(There is one other alternative: if you have taken the time, effort and money to thoroughly research both the conscious and sub-conscious decision drivers, identified the critical drivers of the purchase decision process, tightly defined your audience, found a truly creative person to create the communications, you might make a big impact with much less money.)

But, unless you have a very big budget, integrate those marketing communications to support a few critical, key marketing messages. Perhaps just the most important one.

Failure #8: Process Management

Whether baking a cake or building an office tower, the end product is much better if you follow the correct process. Marketing communication is not any different.

Process is critical.

You have to follow the right steps—in the right order—and perform all the steps.

Here is a typical situation. A product manager wants to prepare a brochure. So, what's the first thing he does? He grabs a piece of paper, folds it in half to make a dummy and draws a circle on the front, labeling it, "dramatic photo." Then he pencils in a title, something clever, like, "Our product—the best in the world."

Opening it up, he pencils in where he wants to talk about feature A, then feature B, and so on until he has the inside pages filled and most of the back, saving room for a phone number and address. Now he just needs a copywriter and artist, and then off to the printer.

This is a disaster.

The sales force, or whoever is to use the brochure will use it to line their trunk or, perhaps a bird cage. The person who's supposed to read it, will glance at it and, at best, file it, but more likely toss it.

Your company has just wasted the cost of this and demonstrated your ignorance of the market. Knowledge of the process and the discipline to follow it would result in a brochure that would help you grow.

Here are the problems he's caused:

Who is he writing to? (Failure #1) Instead of focusing on the reader he's focused on the product. Guarantee—this will be boring. And definitely not convincing. He needs to write with a specific audience in mind—a homogeneous audience.

For example, if he's the manager on laptops, the brochure he prepares for IT personnel should probably be different than the one he writes for the typical laptop user which will probably be different than the brochure he prepares for the college student. And if he tries to write one brochure to all three audiences he'll end up writing a brochure to no audience whatsoever.

And what is his objective? (Failure #2)

Is it to highlight a new product development? Or is he trying to counter a competitive threat in the marketplace? Or has he found out that there is a misperception in the marketplace that he needs to correct?

Well if you don't know where you're going any road will get you there, and if the marketing communications task does not have an objective no road gets you nowhere.

After defining the audience and the objective, next is to consider what to say. (Failure #3) What will move the needle? What is the core promise? What is the support?

This is that marketing decision based on an intimate knowledge of the market and what it values.

After determining what to say, our product manager will finally get to where he originally started out.

How should he say it? (Failure #4)

This is the creative part. How can he phrase his thoughts such that they attract attention? That they are memorable? That they not only interest the reader, but persuade the reader? Believably?

What separates great writers from good writers is their ability to create unique and memorable ways to express a thought. Marketing communications cannot be successful if it's boring or dull. It needs to convey confidence, enthusiasm, and care about the reader.

Marketing communications should reflect those same personality factors that you look for in a salesperson—energy, excitement, trust, knowledge.

Your product manager may exemplify these traits but not have the writing skills necessary to convey them to his audience.

The final issue is to determine where to say it. In advertising parlance this is a media decision. And the temptation to start the process thinking about media can be overwhelming. If our product manager has not started the process with "How to say it," he has started with media. To convey the thought does the product manager need to run a television commercial or supply sales people with a brochure or make a highly targeted mailing? All too often, once again, our product manager starts with this issue.

And he's invariably wrong.

Why? The marketing communications community is rife with media fads. What's the latest thing? What's hot? In the 1990s, everyone had to put together a website. Then everybody had to run banner ads. But this was superseded by search ads. And last year came RSS. And along with this is word-of-mouth and evangelists.

And our product manager is surely up with the fads. Just never learned the basics.

Media decisions can be terribly complicated; but the essential selection criteria revolve around the most efficient method to deliver the message to the audience. Until you've defined the audience and the message you can't really address the media issue.

So, back to the process issue. These are the steps and their order:

1. Who is the audience? (See Failure #1)
2. What is our objective? (See Failure #2)
3. What do we want to say? (See Failure #3)
4. How do we want to say it? (See Failure #4)
5. Where do we want to say it? (See Failure #7)

The right steps—the right order.

Failure #9: Amateurs

Marketing communications managers, advertising managers, PR managers, where do they come from? There are school curricula for these titles, even degrees, both undergraduate

The Failure of Marketing

and graduate. And there are people who carry these degrees in the job. But there are many, many more "professionals" who just fell into the job. And much of the wasted money, irritating communications, failed programs can be tied to the systems that put them in place.

This is not to say that all those with degrees are good and those without are terrible. But Vegas would set the odds that way.

It is not necessarily the fault, though, of the person in the job. A good part of the problem rests, as I pointed out, with the system that put him there.

Joe is a great guy, the other sales guys like him, his manager likes him. But he can't sell. Not at all. Nothing. But no one wants to fire him. Oh no. Not me.

So, there's an opening in advertising. Let's put him in it. Hey, he knows the products inside and out. Are we going to offer him training? Perhaps some immersion courses, association memberships where he can take a few classes? You're kidding aren't you? He'll pick it up. He's a smart guy, just can't sell.

Or the new PR manager comes from Human Resources. She can write; she's personable; she knows the company inside and out. What more does she need to know?

Or . . .

We hired a new ad manager from Acme. He's the one who created that great campaign for them. He can do it for us. Boy, it really put them on the map.

So he approaches one of the product managers with his first recommendation. He thinks it's great and has sound planning, background and reasons for it. But the product manager isn't sure. And it's his budget. So, he takes it home to review it out of the atmosphere of the office. His wife hates it.

147

The next afternoon he tells the ad manager he just doesn't think it will work. Not sure why, but he won't approve it.

The ad manager goes to the VP Marketing. The VP talks with the product manager. The product manager says. "It's my budget. I want to see alternatives. I don't like it and I won't pay for it."

The VP goes back to the ad manager and says he has to come up with alternatives. No suggestion as to what they should be, just a few alternatives. Is that so hard?

In the agency community, it's well known: Clients get the work they deserve.

If you let the amateur make the decision, your chance of good, effective work, communications that move the market, are slim. But, it was your idea to let the amateur make the decision. Don't complain about amateur efforts. Don't fire the agency. Either allow the amateur the training to become professional or find someplace else for him and hire a professional to make the decisions.

Failure #10: Support the Sales Force

This is a special case of Failure #2: Setting objectives. But, while we're bashing senior management we might as well get all their issues out.

So, why do you spend so much on marketing communications?

> To support our great sales force.

And how does it do that?

> It gets our name out. It generates inquiries. It reinforces our message. And then our guys can get in and close the sale.

The Failure of Marketing

Oh, I'll bet the sales guys love it. Let's hear what they have to say. So, guys tell me, I'll bet those inquiries really help, right?

> They're terrible. Bad phone numbers, addresses, no buying influence. A total waste of our time. Don't even bother to follow up on them anymore.

> In fact, from my experience, my customers don't really read our ads. A waste of money. Do you have any idea of what we could do with that money if we had it in our budget?

This is typical of the company where marketing is subordinate to sales. They will never have marketing communications that perform a recognized, valuable function in the company. The entire function is a waste. Marketing has been delegated to each of the sales people. There is no coordinated, customer-focused consistent marketing. Here's a real example:

> We met the client, a $5 Billion company, when they fired their past agency and started to seek a new one. What were their marketing communications objectives? To generate inquiries. That's what the VP of Sales and Marketing wanted. Inquiries.

> We asked the marketing communications manager how he processed the inquiries. We were rather surprised by his answer. His department sent out requested material (this is pre-internet) and then filed the inquiries. He had 27 4-drawer file cabinets loaded with past inquiries. Not one of them had been sent to the sales force.

> They did not want them. Emphatically did not want them.

> A total waste of time.

Several years ago, the new marketing communications manager started sending the inquiries to the sale force. Seemed like a logical thing to do. Perhaps one of their customers had inquired. But the sales force complained to the VP Sales who directed the marketing communications manager to never send one out to the field force again.

Ever.

The same VP who had told us that the advertising must generate more inquiries.

Why? Well, to support the sales force.

What more can I say?

And What About That Sales Force?

What is the role of that sales force? To make sales. Right? Not exactly—in our marketing company.

The fundamental objective of marketing is to create and nurture customer relationships. Nothing can be more powerful than the sales force—when properly trained, directed and supported with the right tools. And, conversely, nothing can be more destructive than a poorly trained, misdirected and unsupported sales force.

First, let's consider the sales force—what it can do and what it can't.

> They can visit customers.
> They can listen to customers.
> They can question customers.
> They can understand what customers say.
> They can talk to customers.

They can talk to the company—management, customer service, product development and the other marketing functions.

That's about it. They listen and they talk.

All they can do is listen and talk. Communicate. And they're talking about marketing.

They must be part of marketing communications.

But they are always considered something special, something apart. The romance of the sales force. Out there on the front lines. Eye-to-eye with customers. Working in remote places, always on the go. Facing rejection at every turn. And easily measurable every day.

What have you sold for me lately? The first thing sold is the salesman.

They come into HQ for a quick visit. Those heroes who are usually only a voice on the phone. They're the ones who meet with the customers, face-to-face, who close those deals that validate the efforts of everyone back at the company.

What are those customers like? What do they like about our products? Was it a tough sell?

The stuff legends are made of.

And when you dig into companies that have been around for awhile, you always hear about legendary figures—and they're usually sales people.

But, not to demean them, all they really do is communicate.

Their communication, though, is a stronger communication than any other marketing activity other than the performance of your product.

151

Why?

It's personal. There is someone in front of you who is delivering the message—live. The customer sees his face, his body language. The customer can ask questions and get a ready answer. The sales person can also ask questions to determine what your company can do to make the customer's life better. This sales person is an extremely powerful communications tool, much more powerful than any ad, website or direct mailer.

Great sales people—go read their books—always recognize the critical importance of establishing relationships with their customers. That great sales person knows that his purpose is to create and nurture customer relationships.

And turn those relationships into sales.

In all too many companies, that's the role of relationships—turn them into sales. Still focused on transactions in the end.

How to change this?

In a true marketing organization directed at building long-term healthy relationships the success of the sales force is based on management. There are three management alternatives:

1. The focus is on transactions. Sell, sell sell.

2. The focus is on relationships because they lead to sales.

3. The focus is on customer growth that results in relationships that lead to mutual growth.

The difference between the three is founded on the attitude of management toward the customer.

Here is the first case: the customer is an adversary, someone to be sold, the sales job sucks.

Consider the car salesman. He knows that everyone walking into the showroom considers him a cheat, a crook, an adversary. He's not there to help you, only to try to get as much money from you as possible.

This is one terrible job.

Then there is the second style: he's focused on the top line. Sales—transactions. Oh, sure, he will defend his relationships. He stresses every day with every sales person the need to build relationships.

Read that McKay book; find out the names of their spouse, children. Play golf, take them to dinner, buy them a drink, take 'em to a play. You want to do business with your friends, right?

But once you have the order, off you go. There is no desire for a longer term relationship. Just close that sale. Get that cash. Build the top line.

And then there's our third case, the sales person who's part of a well structured marketing team, building a relationship by helping the customer and reaping the rewards.

It's not what I can get out of you but what can I do to help you.

The sales person who understands his job as establishing and nurturing a relationship with you, though, is trying to help you. And when successful, he's liked by you and his company. This is a great job.

This sales person's job is much different. He is the point person in building the relationship. But he realizes that the company's goal is to find ways to help the customer meet his goals. And from that intimate understanding his company will grow with the customer.

The difference between the three is obvious; the reason for the differences is due to the attitude of management.

Management calls the shots. Management determines if the sales force is to be a credit to the company or just one more marketing failure.

What kind of sales force do you want?

Finally, sales people are part of marketing communications. All of marketing communications needs to be integrated (see Failure #5). You can't have your sales force promising one thing while your web site makes a contradictory offer. Everybody, every activity has to pull together.

This means communication between sales and marketing. Mutual respect. Mutual understanding of goals and activities. And the sales organization needs to understand their role and the critical role of the relationship.

Failure #11: Meaningful Measurement

Do you measure what you manage or do you manage what you measure?

I have always suspected that the reason managements tend toward transaction thinking, is that it's easy to manage. Back when Henry Ford II was running Ford, every morning on his desk his executive assistant had placed a 3X5 card with the number of cars sold, the number of cars manufactured and the number of cars ordered the previous day.

Easy numbers.

If the auto companies were more focused on customers rather than cars, they might want a few more numbers:

Number of customers
Number of new customers
Complaints to customer service
Number of repeat sales
Number of referrals from existing customers
Warranty repairs

Too many marketers settle for useless measurements:

Aided awareness
Unaided awareness
Information requests
Website Hits
Search optimization

And other executional measurements. But these measurements are directed more at justifying a marketing budget in a company dedicated to transactions than relationships.

Companies focused on transactions will always have a difficult time measuring the value of their marketing communications. For most businesses (with notable exception of retailers, consumer package goods and direct response) sales transactions directly correlate only to sales calls. And that correlation is not always perfect.

Communications directed at transactions have to be focused on buying events—sales, promotions, special deals and the like. Only then are they measurable. This is fine for retailers. But for the remaining 98% of businesses with longer sales cycles, the need for more sales assistance, communication tied to transactions doesn't work.

You can't promote a sale on the steel beams for an office building, or custom plastic moldings or IT services.

"Special this week . . . Steel beams."

And this has become the number one challenge of marketing communications. The CEO and CFO are under so much pressure for efficient management that any significant expenditure must justify itself. What's its ROI?

Marketing communications in a sales environment will have a close to impossible task.

When you build your marketing communications around an overall marketing objective of creating and nurturing customer relationships, you can create measurable communications objectives easier. You have solid, measurable marketing objectives to serve as you center point.

> How do your communications support creating new customers?

> How do your communications support nurturing existing customers?

For example, if you're building your customer relationship around providing the absolutely best service:

> How aware are your non-customers of your high level of service?

> Are your current customers aware of recent service enhancements?

Now you have communications objectives that lead directly to your marketing objectives. They are measurable and have value because the value of a customer is not just the profit from a transaction but of a string of growing transactions into the future. The customer relationship becomes much more valuable. From this you can create an ROI for each of the activities based on the objectives.

This will take you a long way to justifying your budgets.

But this only works if your marketing is focused on relationships.

Failure #12 and The Greatest One of All: The Failure to Live Up to Your Promise.

So, you've done everything right. Nailed it.

Audience—objectives—message—wording—media—integration—sales force alignment—even measurement.

Everything done just right.

The sales into distribution go well.

And the campaign breaks.

The sell-through is terrific.

For a few weeks.

Then the whole program screeches, yes, screeches to a stop.

And returns start.

Distribution is getting angrier each passing minute.

The cost of the returns is proving enormous.

What has happened?

You didn't tell the truth.

The buyer had high expectations—too high.

Your product was great—but not up to the expectations.

Jack Trytten

Now you have to repurchase everything
you sold to distribution.

And your credibility with both
distribution and the market—
Sucks.

This is a company-killer.

Customer relationships require honesty. Real promises you
can keep.

Chapter 9

Price

Now comes the fourth "P", pricing. This is where you're rewarded for all the work you've done in the prior 3 Ps. Setting your price is hard. How do you set a price that adequately rewards you while maintaining—perhaps even enhancing—your relationship with your customer?

Looking through a variety of marketing books, whether basic or advanced the authors all agree on one thing:

Pricing is an art.

Why an art? Because they can't figure out a systematic way to set prices. And art sounds much better than calling it "a shot in the dark" or a "guess."

What's the right price? How do you find it?

The books also offer three basic approaches to setting prices:

1. Cost plus, which comes in two versions
2. Competitive pricing
3. User value

The debates over the best method of the three started with the first marketing textbook and will continue well past our time. The problem with the debate is that the debaters have spent too much time in the classroom and not enough time in the market.

First, each of these methods has their place. But it's not quite the place you think it is.

Second, and most important, you don't set your price. The consumer does.

> The price is the grade the consumer awards you for the value you offer.

You can set your price anywhere, by any rationale you choose. But the consumer, the one paying the price is the one who determines whether or not to pay it.

Start the analysis at the beginning.

When considering price the traditional mind-set is at the transaction. By the time you've read to here, you should now be thinking relationship with the consumer.

Now your analysis has a totally different referent.

In a relationship, the consumer should want to pay the price you set.

They should be happy about this price. That doesn't necessarily mean low price. If it did, the low-priced product would have the entire market. Dunkin' Donuts can tell you this isn't true.

This may also sound suspiciously like user value pricing—but it's not. User value pricing is based on the functionality of a product.

What's the functional value of a Bentley? Of a Grande Latte at Starbucks?

The values of these products depend on the intangibles, the "something else."

It's pricing based on your intimate understanding of your consumer, your buyer.

Your understanding of the "something else." The intangibles.

You also need to consider your overall strategy. Going back to Chapter 6, *Strategy*, there are three generic strategies and they become critical at this point:

1. Quality
2. Quality for a niche
3. Low cost.

Most marketers are pursuing some derivation of strategies 1 or 2. And as pointed out in the discussion on strategy, quality is defined by the consumer.

Let's take a look at a simple situation, cheese purchased as an appetizer for a small party.

Kraft built their business on quality. They are the acknowledged quality leader in basic cheese. Not gourmet cheese though. That's strategy #2, quality for a niche market, in this instance, the gourmet who doesn't even purchase his cheese at the same retailer. He goes to a specialty store or Whole Foods, one with hundreds of different cheeses that cheese experts sample and individually cut for you.

The gourmet stores have set a price. A high price. And understanding the intangibles, they realize that for many who have the money, the higher the price, the "better" the cheese.

Kraft cannot play in this market. But the low end of this market defines for them where the high end of their market is.

And just as there is a high-end niche, there is a price market. Perhaps the college student inviting some friends over to his room for a bottle of wine. Will he splurge for some Kraft cheese or go with a price brand? Probably the price brand.

And the Kraft price becomes the referent for what is a price brand. Kraft doesn't want to compete in this market.

For those of you in the B2B markets, consider a few other products. Laptop computers. Go back about ten years. IBM was the high-end, high-priced brand, serving the very large company, often financially driven with a strong IT department. HP tended to find a niche in the engineering-focused company while Dell and to a lesser degree, Gateway, targeted the more price conscious.

Just as many B2B marketers have built their business based on their understanding of the "something else" in their product, they have learned to price accordingly.

Pig Spill Containment Socks. Until these came along, maintenance used sand, sawdust and a variety of other products to contain spills. New Pig introduced their products, charged a premium price and got it.

How about Kenworth and Peterbuilt trucks?

Caterpillar? Boeing?

All succeed through a mastery of the intangibles.

It's Part of the Product

Why is a Rolls Royce so expensive? Why is a Kenworth truck so expensive? Why is a Starbucks latte so expensive?

Because they wouldn't be what they are if they weren't. The price is part of the product.

When the swarthy gentleman comes up behind you and in whispers offers you a Rolex at a very attractive price, what's wrong? Is it hot? Is it a fake?

When the price over the internet is so low, what's the deal? Is this genuine or a scam?

The price is part of the product.

Part of the attraction of the Ferrari is that it's so expensive. It says I've made it. Look at me. I can afford a $250,000 car that can go, I'm told, almost 200 mph while I live in the city with a speed limit of 30 mph.

The Bentley, the Starbucks coffee, the broach from Tiffany's, they all make the buyer feel special. And we all want to feel special. Give special gifts.

If they weren't expensive, they wouldn't be the same product.

It's the intangibles again, the "something else."

And this can be most mundane. Consider this.

On the left is your basic vegetable peeler. Not exactly an exciting product. Probably not too high on your birthday gift list. It's available at most grocery stores for about $1.69.

Easy to use. Lasts forever. A fine, if utilitarian, piece of kitchen capital equipment.

Now consider the other vegetable peeler.

OXO Good Grips.

Nice rubber handle. The original design was inspired by the problems the wife of the company's founder experienced due to her arthritis. Peeler #1 was painful to use.

Simple fix. A larger, rubberized handle. Easy to grip.

But kind of a niche product—targeted to cooks with arthritis? Right?

And it sells to many, many more people besides the target. OXO has extended the design to most any kitchen gadget you can think of. And many more. OXO has over 500 different products in their current line.

But consider this simple fact.

This peeler will set you back $6.99.

$6.99. Yes, over four times the price of that perfectly utilitarian peeler at the grocery store. 400% plus.

Is OXO's cost four times as much?

Can't be.

Is the competitive price equal?

There is no competition at this price point. (Although there are several other brands even much more expensive.)

Value pricing?

What's the value of a nice soft grip on your peeler—unless you have arthritis? Then, maybe its 400%.

Why are so many people willing to pay 400% more for a simple vegetable peeler? This is not a piece of jewelry. Just a simple kitchen gadget.

If pricing is an art, this is a Rembrandt.

But OXO understands that their products are special. They're special because they make you feel special. When you buy them. When you give them as a gift.

And they are special because of two factors:

> They are thoughtfully designed.
> They are priced to reflect a premium.

In other words, they command a high price because they are high priced.

The consumer has the same trouble you have in evaluating the intangible factors. And a simple way to evaluate them is by considering the price. If it's expensive it must be special.

Starbucks probably wouldn't sell more by reducing its price. Nike probably wouldn't sell more shoes, and OXO wouldn't sell more peelers.

In the B2B world it plays a little different but the end is the same. For example, you may want an air compressor. The one from Ingersoll-Rand is quoted at 10% more than your other choice. Is it worth it? What about the intangibles? You want them.

So you use the quote from company B to leverage a lower price from Ingersoll-Rand. You're still paying more than you would for the other—you could have negotiated with them also.

So How Do You Set Your Price?

It depends.

It depends on your consumer and it depends on your product.

> Does your product make your consumer feel special?
>
> How comparable is your offering on tangible factors?
>
> How about intangible factors? What does the consumer value? How comparable are you with competitors?
>
> Will a higher price add value to the intangibles?

Now set a price. Is your consumer happy paying the price?

If not, change it. Test it, experiment with it.

Let the consumer tell you what your price should be. They're going to set it anyways.

The Failure of Pricing

Keep in mind that your goal in marketing is to build and nurture a relationship with your consumer.

You do that by consistently providing products and services that they value.

The more you make your consumer feel special, the stronger your relationship. And a special price—the right price—makes your consumer feel special. And you too.

It's like getting an "A+" on your marketing test.

Part 4: The Other Failures of Tactics

Oh, so many failures. Depressing.

But just when you thought the 4 P's said it all, come even more.

Just because you manage the basics doesn't mean you're going to have a great customer relationship. There are a few more little skills to master, like:

> The one most irritating, customer service
>
> The one least understood, branding
>
> The one that causes everyone's eyes to glaze over, budgets and measurement
>
> And then the one at the very foundation of all, knowing your buyer and market research.

Fight on.

Chapter 10

Customer Service

Peter Drucker postulated that if your marketing was on target and well-executed, you would have no need for a sales force.

Interesting.

Makes you wonder what he'd think of customer service departments.

What is customer service? Not all companies view this alike. Some companies see it as warranty service, a place to send those who are having problems with their purchase. It's just a place that solve problems so everyone else can get on with business.

Others see it as a place to shuffle off people who just don't get it. We sold it—you bought it. Now don't bother us with your problems.

Others see it as a place to honestly deal with customers' problems and misunderstandings.

A few others see it as a way to make sure their customers feel satisfied with the purchase, a way to build their loyalty and at the same time, learn about how they could improve their offerings.

For most, it's seen as a cost center. But recently, particularly in the computer and software world, it's seen as a profit center.

Profit center.

That is amazing.

Consider, people do not call customer service just to chat. They have a problem, or at least a concern.

This is a potential failure of marketing in the making. Screw up here and you are destroying any chance of creating loyalty.

So how do you handle this?

First, let's consider the problem.

The product doesn't work due to a manufacturing error. Hey, this happens. Six Sigma is pretty good but still it's not absolute in guaranteeing zero manufacturing errors.

Seems a reasonable call. Most of us fix it. Here's a situation with GE. I had purchased a GE microwave that fit under the cabinet above my stove. The turntable stopped running after 8 months. I called the retailer for service, as noted on the receipt, and someone came out and repaired it. But 10 months later it broke again.

Now the retailer quoted a price of $140 over the phone for service as it was out of warranty. Even though this had been the second time for repair.

I called GE customer service. They apologized, said they wished I had called their service initially, but would send a coupon good for the service call anyways.

They didn't know me. I can't imagine I was in any database of heavy user customers. But they wanted to make sure their product made me happy. This was important enough for them to make an exception to the warranty and cover the repair.

They sure built up my appreciation for GE.

Here's another call to customer service.

There is something the caller doesn't understand. She wants some help. Someone to guide her through a process.

This is what stumps so many companies. They think to themselves, it's clearly explained in the manual. Why don't they just read it?

Apparently, they don't because it's easier to call customer service. But when you consider that this is a cost center and all of us have been cutting costs for as long as we can remember, calling customer service is not really all that easy. The phone menus, the waiting for someone to become available. The recorded messages. The music. Calling is really a pain. It's not so easy.

So what the customer is telling you when they call is that your manual is even worse than calling your customer service.

That's pretty bad.

If you really want to save money in customer service, come out with a decent manual.

I purchased a laptop from Dell. A few years later I purchased additional memory from Dell.

When it arrived, the installation instructions weren't clear and pictured a different configuration than what I had.

I called customer service. They wanted $39 before they'd answer my questions. I had no choice. I paid.

A few years later I purchased a new laptop. Then I had a choice. It wasn't Dell. I didn't even consider them.

The computer software industry seems to have taken customer service to new lows.

Consider this experience with Intuit.

I had retained a new accountant and he suggested, strongly, that we do our bookkeeping with Quickbooks. We're a small company with just a few employees and this seemed like a good idea at the time. The program cost about $200 but seemed like a good, efficient and easy-to-use program.

Furthermore, they offered a payroll service that for a few hundred dollars more a year would regularly download up-to-date payroll tax tables which the program would use to figure correct withholding and payroll taxes. Payroll for our few employees was really easy.

All was fine for two years.

Then I got the letter.

I would not be able to subscribe to payroll anymore unless I upgraded to the next version of Quickbooks. In other works, in addition to paying an annual subscription to the payroll service I was going to have to update my program every two years for an additional $200! Looking at it that way, Quickbooks was going to cost me $300 per year.

And it was their way or the highway.

After a heart-to-heart discussion with my accountant I decided not to upgrade. I would figure out withholding and the related taxes using the tables provided by the IRS.

In this process, I discovered something else. While I subscribed to their service, my program downloaded "updated" tables about every other month. Using the tables from the IRS, I have figured out the withholding amounts at the beginning of the year and have never had to "update" them during the year. What was all this downloading about?

About a year later, I switched computers (from Dell to IBM, see above) and had some difficulty installing the program. I called Intuit.

You guessed it. They wanted $39.95 to talk with me.

It's now three years after I started figuring out the withholding on my own. I just received another letter. I had better upgrade because they are stopping all support for my version of the program.

In other words, if you have a problem,

Don't call, don't write.

We don't want to hear from you.

They have turned marketing loyalty entirely around. If they are going to be loyal to me, I had better buy their latest version.

I am buying their loyalty?

Not a chance.

The Customer Service Tipping Point

What a few companies really understand is that when a customer calls with anything, a problem, a question, a concern, a suggestion, you have the opportunity to dramatically increase their loyalty.

The research on this goes back three decades at least and is redone by someone about every three to four years. The results are always the same.

A customer problem handled fairly results in your most loyal customer.

Your *most* loyal customer.

That's the goal.

But if you screw it up, you've lost the customer. Forever.

Both you and your customer would prefer you not need customer service. But that's only going to happen in a perfect world.

We're not even close yet.

Neither you nor your customers are perfect. So you need customer service. And it is right on the edge—

Handled well, you have an extremely loyal customer.

Handled poorly, you create a customer for your competitors.

How important are loyal customers? How much are they worth?

The Positive Side of Customer Service

If your goal is to create loyal customers, customer service can be one of your strongest tools.

This is your feedback loop. This is one of the best ways to find out what your best friends won't tell you.

Customer service tells you where you can improve, add more value.

Consider the earlier comments about calls where the answer was in the manual. Enough calls like this are telling you clearly that you need to improve your manuals. Keep in mind, good manuals can be a strong selling point.

Adobe takes this a few steps further and created their *Classroom in a Book*, a great tutorial series for learning how to use their products. Each course sells for an additional $50. A nice add-on sale for an expensive product.

Tracking of customer service calls have led to product improvements, new products, new services and a host of new business opportunities.

Keep in mind who's calling you.

These people are your friends. Potentially your best friends.

They have already laid out the cash for your product. The cash your company uses to pay your salary; the salary you use to pay your mortgage and put food on the table. Isn't this important?

When you treat them as friends and realize that every call with a problem is an opportunity to improve, perhaps even create a new product, a new business, you must consider customer service way too important to be an afterthought.

The Failure of Customer Service

When it takes longer to get customer service than sales . . .

When customer service doesn't report to marketing . . .

When you outsource customer service to an outside, offshore firm . . .

When you fail to track the reason for the calls . . .

When you fail to listen and learn from the calls . . .

You are failing your customers.

And when you charge them for this . . .

    You are creating a loyal customer for your competition.

Chapter 11

The Brand

During mid-seventies the marketing community, always up for a new fad, jumped on promotions as their new savior.

> Coupons,
> Cents off.
> Two-fers.
> Tie-ins.
> On-packs.
> In-packs.

And on, and on and on.

The new hot firm was the promotion agency. They sprung up like dandelions. And, boy did they make money. So every agency, watching their client budgets drift to these up-starts, started promotion departments, subsidiaries, or affiliates.

And the traditional marketing folks decried the terrible drain on the traditional marketing budget but they had little impact. They were behind the times.

What drove this?

Measurement and apparent incremental sales.

You could count coupons and each represented a sale.

You could see unit sales increase during the promotion. And watch them decrease when your competitors launched theirs.

For the CMO—and particularly for his boss—you could measure. And what you could measure you could manage. This was great.

For a while.

Then, it slowly started to sink in.

Unit sales were not really growing. Number of customers was not growing. Dollar sales were declining.

And those loyal customers were shifting from competitor to competitor.

Who has the best deal today?

Once again, proving that consumers are smarter than marketers.

It took about 10 years for marketers to understand this.

A decade.

What they realized took their breath away.

Their products, once considered special, distinctive, unique, were now that dreaded class, the purgatory of marketing.

The Failure of Marketing

Commodities.

Talk about the failure of marketing; we're there.

And the turnabout was a stampede.

And the new fad sponsored a new name,

Branding.

It was all about the brand.

And every ad agency, promotional agency, every marketing resource paying attention became a branding agency.

And every marketer's resume started out with a commanding statement of ability to build and grow the brand.

Problem was, no two people agreed as to what a brand was.

> To the branding agency née corporate identity firm, branding was the company or product name.

> To the branding agency née design studio, branding was the logo.

> To the branding agency née promotion agency branding was increasing value through tie-ins and cross-promotions.

> To the branding agency née old-fart traditional advertising agency, branding is what they'd been doing all along.

And to CMOs, branding was going to save them from commodity-hell, get them promoted, perhaps even to CEO.

If they could just figure out what branding was.

Because no one could agree. Other than branding was what they did, had been doing, and did better than anyone else.

That was over twenty years ago. During the nineties, David Aaker wrote a series of three books on branding. The seminal thinking.

Apparently no one read them. Branding is still misunderstood and misrepresented.

As recently as 2004, Don E. Schultz, a distinguished marketing communications professor at Northwestern University published *Brand Babble. Sense and Nonsense About Branding.*

What is so hard to understand about branding? Let's find out.

What is a brand?

Very simply,

A brand is the core value the marketer provides to the relationship he has with the consumer. It is a promise.

A few examples:

Coke	Refreshment
Volvo	Safety
Nordstrom	Great customer service
Southwest	Affordable travel
Hertz	Excellent service
Four Seasons	Impeccable service
Kraft	Reliable, tasty basic foods
McDonalds	Consistent, friendly restaurant experience

The brand is the core value. Marketing adds additional values that are not necessarily part of the brand. For example, Coke is available just about everywhere, grocery stores, restaurants, convenience stores, lunch rooms. This is great distribution, but not part of the brand.

Coke is also available in a multitude of sizes. Also not part of the brand.

A brand is a promise to the consumer. The core, critical promise. But a brand does not encompass the consumer expectations. That is the product's reputation.

Branding is not naming. Naming is part of branding as it makes little sense to promote a value without associating it with your name.

Branding also is not a logo. Although a good logo is helpful to associate the name with the brand promise.

A good brand lasts a long time. For example:

Coke	Since the 1920's
Volvo	Since the 1950's
Southwest	Since their inception in 1971

Once again, a brand is a promise of a core value.

The Failure of Branding

While the inability of so many marketers to understand the concept of branding is an obvious failure, there's an even bigger one, one much more important:

The failure of the marketer to understand the values of the consumer.

Nothing is quite as pathetic as the marketer extolling a promise that the consumer doesn't value.

And it happens all too frequently. Consider,

Ford—	Bold Moves.
American Airlines—	We know why you fly.
Pepsi—	It's the cola

Citibank—	Banking the way it should be
Sheraton—	Belong
Panasonic—	Ideas for life

Do you believe these promises? Are they compelling? Do they touch at the core reason for their customer relationship? They look like slogans to me. Just slogans, not sincere promises that form the foundation of a customer relationship.

So what's the difference?

All marketers want relationships. But only a few smart ones spend the time and money to find out what their customers really want, what drives their purchase decision.

What's at the core.

They build their offerings around their customers' values, and continually work to maintain or grow their value.

You have to know the core value of your product or service to the customer. And then deliver it better than your competitors.

That's branding.

Chapter 12

The Battle for the Budget—Measurement

Take off your marketing hat and put yourself in the place of the VP—Production. He has found a way to save almost $200,000 a year. However, this will take an investment of almost $1 million. The payback is great, a little more than 5 years.

He takes this to the CFO. Wonderful, a simple ROI of 20%. But where to get the $1 million? It's just not lying around.

Look at that marketing budget. They're spending almost $30 million on media advertising a year. What's their ROI? Can they even calculate one?

And once more, Marketing takes the hit.

The screaming need in the marketing world for the past 10 years has been to justify the marketing expenditures, particularly the media costs, based on the traditional financial tools.

Good luck.

In the old, tired transactional marketing model, this led to direct mail, direct response, coupons, promotions and other activities that were easily measurable, or so the marketing world thought at the time.

They woke up when they finally realized they had sold their brand value down the drain. They'd paid for all these promotions by stealing the dollars from the advertising that supported their brand promise.

They paid—and still are paying—big time for this. And the CMO, CFO and CEO are now caught in a terrible spot. They know they need brand support but have no way to figure its return.

So, what have they done? How have they tried to justify the dollars?

Inquiries. What's the value of an inquiry?

Measure the funnel, you know:

Awareness ➔ familiarity ➔ comprehension ➔ preference ➔ purchase.

What's the value of each of the steps? How much does it cost to move from one to the next?

Can we just take a financially less rigorous approach? Can we just say our expenditure is necessary for $XX of sales?

The Measurement Failure

This is simple. All these attempts are doomed to fail as they are trying to relate a long-term, strategic activity to a moment in time, a transaction.

On the other hand, if you accept that the role of marketing is to create and nurture customer relationships, then you can measure the value of your overall marketing based on the value of your relationships.

The lifetime value of a customer relationship.

Simply calculated, this is the profit from a customer over the lifetime of the relationship or:

Profit per transaction x number of transactions per year x number of years.

Now you need to consider those activities you must take to maintain that relationship.

How much new product R&D?

How much communication to attract the customer in the first place?

How much communication to attract additional customers as they come into the market?

How much for customer service?

How much for personal relationship management (sales personnel)?

How much for a website that offers user hints and tips?

How much for all those other marketing activities necessary to maintain the relationship?

That's your total marketing cost.

For an ROI analysis:

Total value of all the customer relationships for the year less the total marketing costs divided by the total marketing cost.

Think about that for a moment. Calculate that in your head quickly, roughly.

The ROI is going to be huge. And it's the only true ROI.

It's the only one that really generates revenue. All the others just reduce cost.

Consider that before you slash that marketing budget.

Oh, but oh, can't you reduce that huge marketing cost? What about that great big media budget?

Here's the basic problem. Marketing, particularly well-conceived and managed marketing, is a system.

It's a system.

Let's take a simple system. A car.

What's the value of the front tire on the driver's side? If you don't have one, it's the value of the car.

That's the problem with systems. If one of their parts goes, the whole thing goes right with it.

The challenge in managing this system for maximum efficiency is in understanding the nature of the relationship. To do that, you need to understand the total value proposition, particularly the intangibles, the "something else."

If you think of your marketing as the courting and eventual life-time relationship you have with your spouse, you will begin to identify those critical activities that form the basis of the relationship.

How did you meet? What did you want to know? How do you relate now? What do you talk about? What joint activities do you value? What and how much do you share? What do you care about? What can the other do to make you feel wonderful?

As you translate relationship values to your own marketing you'll begin to appreciate how important different activities are.

And when you really, fully develop a comprehensive understanding of your customer relationship, you'll know how to maximize the efficiency of your marketing system.

Chapter 13

Customer Knowledge

Sitting across the desk from my first client, I was stunned when the VP Sales told us he knew every customer who could possibly purchase his company's products. Every single customer.

Wow, was this guy smart or what?

Events over the next two months proved him wrong. Not just a little wrong, but way wrong. Our efforts uncovered enough new prospects to double the sales of two of their products and triple—triple—the sales of one more.

His faulty market knowledge was very expensive. The new prospects resulted in a sales increase of over 40%, requiring they expand their plant almost 25%. These were not new

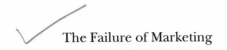

products. Our client just had not considered these prospects as needing their products.

Knowledge of customers is critical for successful marketing:

> Marketing strategy, building customer relationships, requires accurate and intimate customer knowledge.

> Building product value requires you know what customers value.

> Managing distribution requires you know where customers are and their values.

> Promotional dialogue requires you know who they are and what they value.

> Price is dependent entirely upon customer knowledge.

> Customer service depends on customer knowledge, and generates it also.

> Branding, same thing: requires customer knowledge.

This may seem repetitious but the point can't be stressed enough.

Successful marketing is entirely dependent on accurate, timely, comprehensive and intimate customer knowledge.

It is the basic raw material, the input, for marketing.

Not assumptions. Knowledge.

Not guesses. Knowledge.

Real, honest-to-Pete knowledge.

No substitutes.

Jack Trytten

So Where Does This Knowledge Come From?

The sales force?

Not quite. Most sales personnel are tactically oriented. And they understand their job well. It's to generate sales. Generating and assimilating customer knowledge is, at best, secondary, in a job that has no secondary time or effort.

Buy they provide knowledge anyway. Loosely.

"Here's how I sold the last customer. Here's why we lost the last bid. Here's why I captured this customer from that competitor. Here's why we lost the other one."

Solid tactical information. One data point at a time.

Not only usually unhelpful but often highly misleading.

If you are to have intimate customer knowledge, you must have an organized, systematic and thorough process dedicated to it.

So you turn to market research.

Which comes in two flavors:

1. Qualitative—which tells you why

2. Quantitative—which tells you how many

And you need them both.

Qualitative without quantitative tells you why but basing plans on "why" without "how many" risks chasing a small market with major resources. Risky.

Quantitative without qualitative tells you "how many" but not "why". So you guess. And often guess wrong.

192

You need them both if you are to really know your market.

But, you say, we do use them both and we're still often wrong. (Consider that 80% of new products fail.)

Several Minor Failures of Market Research

It's simple. Market research often provides wrong information, incomplete information, or misleading information.

And these can often be expensive mistakes. You don't haul out the big research guns until you have a major issue. While market research is expensive, the risk in the market is even bigger.

But this all seems so simple. If you want to know the time, you ask. If you want to know if they like your product, can't you also just ask?

No.

Here's where it all goes wrong. First, problems with qualitative research:

Most users of qualitative research opt for focus groups. The only other alternative is some form of one-on-one interviews which are even more expensive and time consuming. Are there problems with focus groups?

Take off your marketing hat, go home, have dinner with your spouse and family. After dinner your phone rings. Someone inviting you to participate in a focus group. Pays $150 for two hours after work.

Sure, why not. You have the time and the money would be nice.

And you walk in to the facility after a busy day at work to meet nine total strangers.

Who are they? What do they do? What are they like? Any customers here? Any neighbors?

You introduce yourself. And while you're sitting out in the reception room, having a light dinner, you begin to chat, ask questions, be questioned. And you are evaluating the group—and being evaluated. The young guy is an accountant—boooooring. The older fellow is a retail store assistant manager. The woman is a high-class clerk of some kind, and the other two aren't talking much but from the casual way they're dressed, probably don't make much money.

You are a captain of industry, responsible for multi-million dollar budgets and the management of a team of twenty.

And so the evening goes.

There are leaders, followers and revolutionaries. A few hardly talk at all, either intimidated or just too dull to have anything to add or don't care.

Now back to your marketing hat. Do you really think these people, including you, really opened their hearts and minds to the moderator? Do you think your comments as "captain of industry" had any impact on what others then said?

Absolutely!

And there's another problem. It's called priming. Each of us has a genetic predisposition to please authority figures. And the moderator is an authority figure. Try as he or she might to disguise the purpose of the research, the group will figure out the issues and guess at the "right" answers. They may guess wrong but it changes their answers. They want to please the moderator.

Except for those few who have "issues" with authority who try to not please the moderator.

Either way, the answers don't necessarily reflect the true feelings of the individuals in the group.

You cannot deny or obviate the social dynamics of a group. For basic exploration of ideas, focus groups often generate false information. Very often.

False research. That leads to expensive mistakes.

Second, how we make purchase decisions is complicated. We'll go into this in more detail in a later chapter but the key at this point is to recognize that all decisions involve subconscious drivers, typically considered emotional. All purchase decisions.

Truthfully now, are you comfortable talking about your emotions in a group of ten strangers? I know I'm not.

More false research.

Now on to surveys. We want to find out how many.

Surveys are for counting noses. They are typically conducted by telephone, mail, in-person and recently, over the internet.

But like focus groups, surveys commonly suffer from two flaws,

> How many what?

> Why? Maybe because of . . . ?

Surveys by definition are composed of set questions that are posed to the respondents the same way. Which requires critical assumptions on your part:

1. That you anticipate the possible interpretations of the wording of your question.

2. That you anticipate all the possible responses that the respondent might make or wish to make.

For example, you may ask respondents to rank factors, such as, "Which of these five factors is the most important?"

What if the most important factor is not on the list?

It happens all too often.

But the worst mistake of the survey is after looking at the numbers, guessing as to why.

Here's an example.

A survey of people attending an event returned the following results for a question on household income:

< $50	39%
$50 - $75	13%
$76 - $100	32%
> $100	16%

Is this a normal distribution of income? How should this be interpreted?

Looking at similar data from the same event 5 years later,

	2001	2006
< $50	39%	34%
$50 - $75	13%	13%
$76 - $100	32%	35%
> $100	16%	18%

Obviously, our sample has had a nice increase in income. Why?

> Because they are having good years?
> Because they are older, and older people have higher incomes?
> Because the event is attracting a wealthier audience than before?

Because ticket prices have significantly increased?

It could be any of those, and I'm sure you can hypothesize more. But that's all they are, hypotheses.

You don't know. But did you think to ask in the second event if those people had been at the first event? Did you ask their age? Did you ask the second group what their income had been 5 years earlier?

No. So you aren't going to be able to tell.

And if this is important knowledge, you have two options:

Guess

Go back and ask more questions.

Here's the test of how good a marketing person you are:

If you guess, you're not

If you go back and ask, you are.

A true marketer will never hesitate to ask more questions. The only hindrance is the willingness of the respondents to participate in the dialogue. And the mark of a good researcher is the ability to extend that dialogue until your knowledge of your customers is intimate.

The Huge Mistake with Market Research

Why do you only use market research when you have a major issue? How much do you spend on trying to understand, anticipate, know your competition?

If you are to have truly great marketing—consistently—you shouldn't treat market research as an "every now and then" activity.

You should always be in the market asking questions, learning, developing a more intimate understanding of your customer.

This should be as natural and consistent as breathing.

How many marketers do it?

A client at a major (huge) packaged goods manufacturer made it a habit to call 2 to 3 consumers every day. Just to chat.

What was on their minds? How were their activities changing? What was right in their world? What was wrong?

10 to 15 people a week. Over 500 a year. A lot of people.

And he knew the market so well, and understood the dynamics, what was changing and why, that his products grew faster than his competitors'. He always had good ideas for new products. He always anticipated what he needed to do to improve his product.

His consumers were the most important people in his work world. He felt he needed to know them very well—intimately.

It paid off.

Part 5: Great Marketing

"Let me tell you about the very rich. They are different from you and me."

F. Scott Fitzgerald, 1926

Let me tell you about the great marketers. They are very different, also. But the differences are subtle. Seemingly small. But oh, so important.

Here's what makes them different. And great.

Chapter 14

Why Customers Buy

The core of marketing, the absolute essence, is the understanding of why your customers buy.

What do they value? What are they considering? Just what goes through their mind?

A consistent, accurate and comprehensive understanding.

If you understand, you are well on your way to avoiding failure.

Unfortunately, understanding is not as simple as just asking.

It is, to a degree, brain surgery.

Consider that marketing is about either changing behavior, the action of those who are not customers, or maintaining behavior, the action of those who are.

Simply, marketing is about behavior.

There is science to this, psychology. This is the foundation of marketing just as mathematics is the foundation of engineering. Every marketing person should have grounding in psychology just as every engineer has a foundation in mathematics.

Psychology has been undergoing a revolution for the past twenty years, starting slowly. The changes in the past few years with the emergence of functional magnetic resonance imaging (fMRI) have completely revolutionized thinking about how we make decisions.

This has led to a greater understanding of the purchase decision.

An Obsolete Way of Thinking

About 350 BC, Plato and Aristotle "created" rational man. Western thought has not been the same since.

Rationality is good—irrationality is bad.

And western man was to become the ultimate rational thinker. Right.

Over the centuries these ideas became grossly perverted to lead marketers well astray.

> Careful, reasoned, rational decisions = good.

> Quick, emotional decisions = bad.

Our marketing thinking is littered with pseudo-psychological descriptions of purchase behavior:

> Considered purchase
> Impulse purchase
> Habitual purchase
> And so on . . . .

Throw all this out. Obsolete. Yesterday's news.

This is the thinking that leads to a greater than 80% failure rate in new product development. This thinking leads to maddening customer service. It is responsible for a bevy of marketing failures. The failure of marketing itself.

It is now time for marketing to catch up with what the psychologists, biologists, neuroscientists, and cognitive scientists have known for quite some time.

This is not how we make decisions.

Your Brain on Marketing

Your brain has several decision-making processes. At one extreme is what you have been calling "rational", that is your conscious decision process. You weight values, alternatives and come to a conclusion. Actually, it doesn't work quite like that but we'll cover that later.

At the other extreme, the reptilian mind, you have the process that decides how often and when you should breath, your heart rate and so forth. Right above that is the control of your voluntary muscles, the process that controls your hand when you're reaching for the next Bud Light.

You really don't have to think about these processes. They are subconscious.

Also subconscious is the process that should become near and dear to your marketing heart. It's where you make decisions such as, " . . . should you really have that Bud Light."

It's the same process that causes you to feel uncomfortable should you forget something as you walk out the door. The same process that results in your remembering the name of that actor in the old B-movie that you couldn't remember a few minutes ago.

203

Surely you've had this experience. You've left work with something on your mind. You get to your car, start it, drive home and as you pull into the garage you realize you don't remember even driving home. That's the process.

It's a subconscious process and it's wonderful. It's a great decision-maker. Here's how it compares to your conscious decision process:

1. Speed: The conscious process is slow. The subconscious is lightning fast.

2. Complexity: The conscious process must rely on short-term memory. It works fine with up to seven variables and slows down after that, crashing at about 15 variables. The subconscious can handle, well, lots more. Over thirty, with no sweat.

3. Explicitness: The conscious mind will let you articulate explicitly why you made the decision. The best the subconscious will do is to tell you it "felt right." It's often called your gut.

Now, here's the neat part. They are both constantly working and they work together. As a result, we humans have the best decision-making skill of any animal. But it's complex.

This has created enormous problems for our market researcher. Essentially, your subconscious is suggesting a decision and your conscious is double-checking it. But when our researcher comes along and asks you why you made that decision, your conscious takes over, ignoring the subconscious. It offers a hypothesis. A guess. And one reasonable answer, if only a guess, is often enough.

Something Else

Back in Chapter 6 on the product, I pointed out that much of what drives the purchase is a "something else." Now the time has come to elaborate on what that is.

We purchase products and services because they help us in our lives. But how they do that is often not obvious, not to us as researchers or even to us as purchasers. Sometimes you just have to probe among the functional. For the ITW Shakeproof SEMS® screw and washer, the advantage was functional but not the obvious. While it eliminated a dreary, tedious assembly step, it also and more importantly cut down on warranty costs from parts falling off. The warranty savings is what drove the purchase.

More likely though, the something else is tied up in the subconscious and not amenable to simple probing. For example, the brand and model of car you purchase is an expression of how you perceive yourself at the moment of purchase. It is as much an expression of your desired appearance as your clothes.

The purchase of your do-it-yourself tools would seem to be purely functional. However, why you spend more on a DeWalt drill is wrapped up in your subconscious evaluation of your skill, your self-image along with your functional needs.

In short, that "something else" is an amalgam of the subconscious drivers of the purchase decision.

Let's consider this in some detail:

Here are some cordless drills and their prices. They are all top of the line for their brand:

Black & Decker	$79
Skil	79
Ridgid	189
Makita	199
DeWalt	209

Quite a price range and a bit of clumping at the bottom and near the top. All recognized brand names. I would expect them all to be good products. But which one do you pick? Which brand appeals to you?

For those of you with considerable skill in DIY projects you'll probably go for the DeWalt or the Makita. Not just because they're the most expensive although that doesn't hurt, but because those are the most likely ones you'll see on a professional job site. But you'll also realize that you should take a close look at the Skil and Black & Decker because the companies make good solid equipment that may not have the duty cycle for a pro but is fine for occasional home use. You probably aren't using it eight hours a day.

For those of you who have gobs of money and enjoy owning the best, you'll buy the DeWalt.

And for those of you who want to be sure your neighbor knows you're making gobs of money, you'll also buy the DeWalt.

For those who are more modest, more conservative, well, the Skil is just fine. Or maybe the Black & Decker. You have a nice set of tools and you feel you have a reasonable level of skill, certainly not professional but, say, capable.

And for those that are always looking for bargains, you need to wait a few weeks to see what goes on sale.

Some disparage this type of analysis as "ego" but it really relies more on our perceptions of our self. Now there is much greater depth in this analysis but you should get the idea of that "something else." All of these will drill holes. All are 18 volts, ½ inch drills. All work wonderfully well. Pure functionality is not an issue. Three are used by professionals. Two are designed for the DIYer. All are available at Home Depot.

Several years ago I lived next door to a doctor who really enjoyed DIY, always doing something around the house. He had no training, though and his workmanship was not up to amateur standards, much less professional. But he had plenty of money. And he had all the best tools. He enjoyed purchasing them and using them even though the results were less than stellar. What was most interesting, he purchased the tools when he was facing difficult cases. It was one of the ways he dealt with stress—go buy a tool. Buy a good one.

That's really "something else."

Searching for Something Else

So how do you find out? There are a few firms that have developed methodologies to probe the subconscious. The author heads one of those firms. We each employ different approaches. However, we all agree on a few issues:

1. We all use a 1 on 1 approach.

2. It requires very skillful questioning.

3. The interviews take quite a bit of time.

4. Through skillful probing of the subconscious, the respondent eventually tells you exactly how and why the purchase was made. No guessing.

5. The totality of what's learned is so rich, so deep that it often inspires new approaches for new products and services.

6. You can take the results to the bank.

We have used our approach on a wide variety of products and markets. The results have been very accurate. The variety has been huge:

> Food products
> Household products
> Consumer durables
> Industrial capital equipment (yes, you better believe there's a ton of emotion involved)
> Industrial components and materials
> Industrial consumables

We've used this on most everything but fashion and cosmetics. Just haven't had the chance. Yet.

A Simple Example

Our client was concerned about the acceptance of a new air compression technology they were introducing. The technology had been used in very large machines, used in sophisticated applications. Now they were adapting it to smaller applications that would be sold through distribution.

Would the market accept it?

Air compressors had been sold based on energy efficiency since the energy crisis of the 1970s. This was twenty years later. The entire industry was still sold on the basis that their machine was the most efficient. Each had developed a test to prove it—of course, no one used the same test and had solid reasons why theirs was the best.

We visited with 15 plant engineers to talk in depth with them while in their plant, in their comfort zone.

When asked, they all agreed that energy efficiency was important. But when pressed further as we drilled deeper, they revealed the true reason.

While energy efficiency was what they "sold" to senior management, their real reason had little to do with it. This was the key.

Reliability.

Why? It's simple. If the compressor goes down unexpectedly, the portion of the plant it supports goes down with it.

The employees get a free paid holiday. Production slows. Deliveries are late.

The cost of one unexpected shutdown could cost far more than the energy savings over the life of the compressor.

Who would get the blame for this? Which personnel file would hold the report? The plant engineer.

Not good for the career.

Careers trump energy efficiency all day long.

But what's worse for the plant engineer was the thought of having to sell his wife and friends that his career had taken a hit—that he'd been laid off—because of the air compressor he purchased. He was damn well going to make sure it was reliable.

This little, almost obvious, insight led to 20% growth in market share. Not only did the marketing communications change to dramatize reliability, although not featuring a husband explaining to his wife he'd been laid off. But the client reexamined their machines to be sure they were providing the most reliable compressor.

A Much More Complex Example

The food decision is one of the most challenging to research. Your subconscious reactions to food go back to early childhood. Because it is so intimate a product, the subconscious is packed with all types of influences to be sorted through.

We were helping a client develop a flavoring for coffee. This is pre-Starbucks. The product was line of flavorings that were essentially flavored powdered creamers. They tasted great. The challenge was in figuring out what kind of product we were dealing with.

Coffee, at that time, was considered a strictly adult beverage. The "coming of coffee age" happened in the very late teens for college students, somewhat later for the rest of the population.

It was not an easy thing to come to like.

Coffee at its best is bitter. Slightly acidic. Not something most of us take to naturally. Thus cream and sugar.

General Foods had a well-established and successful product with their International Coffee line of instant flavored coffees. Several of the higher end coffee purveyors were starting to introduce flavored beans. Our product seemed to be a good fit with market trends.

All these products were marketing themselves as ways to demonstrate your sophistication to those around you. The GF product had led on this theme for many years.

When we tried this out on focus group attendees, they bought right in. Oh, this is the way to go.

In test market, it failed. So much for focus groups.

We went back at it with more intimate research. The people who really loved our product essentially didn't like coffee.

But they liked the buzz and the idea that they were drinking an adult beverage.

Our product gave them a way to like coffee. Particularly the flavors that turned it into a candy bar. It became a very personal indulgence. It still had the buzz. It was still adult. But it tasted great.

In test market it took off. Same product. Different value proposition.

Where to Find the Answers

The research methodology that uncovers the subtleties of the subconscious take trained psychological interviewing. But through our experiences, we offer a few tips.

First, appreciate that no product should be viewed in isolation. All products have a context. With the compressor it was the overall economy of the plant. With food and many consumer products, they must be viewed within the context of the purchaser's life.

We don't purchase things for what they are but for what they mean to our daily life.

The primary areas to explore are aspirations, beliefs and values.

When you understand those three factors, you understand your market. It will amaze you how easy your marketing will become.

Chapter 15

The Complete Solution

Understanding the drivers of your customer's purchasing decision is critical to marketing success. However, it is not in itself, sufficient. There are a few more critical factors.

Attitude

(A state of mind or a feeling; a disposition.)

By now you have a pretty good idea of how you should develop your marketing strategy and a few ideas of what your tactical approach should be. But there is one more fundamental that is critical to great marketing:

Attitude.

You need to love your customer.

Would it amaze you to know how many senior managers, marketing people hold their customers in some kind of contempt? You see it often at focus groups. The management filters in at the last moment, glances at the list of attendees and the discussion guide. Then, as a customer expresses their viewpoint, contrary to what management "knows", they laugh and call her an idiot. A fool.

These are the people who are paying for your son's college, your daughter's braces, your fishing trip, your wife's new Lexus SUV (and the gas to keep it going).

What's not to love?

To reiterate:

Your goal is not to sell them your product. Your goal is to make them happier, make their life better, delight them.

If you are to do that, you have to care about them. Real, honest, genuine care.

Love.

If you don't, the customer will feel it, eventually know it and gravitate to those who care.

Take the airlines for example. Do the legacy carriers love their customers? Ha! Not a chance. They love their jobs and their positions and their perks.

Customers come last.

Then there's Southwest. "Love" is part of their slogan, and love of their customer is part of their culture. Top to bottom. What's the right thing to do for their customer?

You can feel the difference when you board, when they hand out the snacks, when they wish you a good day. They care and the others don't.

So who's been profitable and who's been through bankruptcy? Where would you like to be?

Attitude: love your customer. Without them you don't have a business.

Whose Attitude?

Yours? The CEO's? Senior management's? Whose attitude?

Everyone's. From the board of director's to the person who sweeps the floor of the factory. Everyone contributes to creation of customer value and everyone has to have the attitude.

They all need to keep in mind that the only sustainable source of money for their paycheck is from the customer.

When Bob Buckman took the reins of Buckman Laboratories from his late father he discovered there was no organization chart. He created one in a unique way; he asked each employee to write their own job description. Who would know better? But, each had to describe their job in terms of how they created customer value.

Brilliant. How many of you consider how you create customer value? What do you do that directly affects customer loyalty?

When you and everyone in your company understand this, value this, you will have the foundation upon to build a great strategy and implement loyalty-building tactics.

Discipline

Marketing, like everything else worth doing, requires discipline.

You are going to face challenges and if you are to maintain your focus on the customer, you had better be willing to face them down. It takes commitment and discipline.

First, you face external challenges. There will always be a few customers who take advantage of you. Fortunately, just a few. It's their personality type. They don't want a relationship, just the benefits. They will negotiate until they feel they have you down to the last nickel. Then use that negotiation to leverage someone else. Really makes you mad.

You just don't deal with them again.

Unfortunately you can't predict who these customers are; you only recognize them as you attempt to build a relationship.

But you can't set your policy, develop your strategy or execute your tactics based on these few. You're basing 100% of your actions on the boorish behavior of 2 to 3%.

Second, you face internal challenges. There are often a few employees who just don't get it. No matter how you try, they just can't bring themselves to embrace the tenets of marketing. For example, a retailer I've worked with is dedicated to the proposition that the customer comes first—always. But they have a few sales associates that just won't embrace that. They'll argue with customers, they'll refuse service when they think the policy is being abused, and otherwise put the store before the customer.

How are they to know the overall value of a particular customer?

Are you going to let a few employees decide to take your policy into their own hands? Who's in charge?

These challenges present difficult situations. But it's better to accept them, to learn from them than pretend they're not there or let a very few ruin a great marketing strategy.

Embrace Change

Embrace change? Of course you embrace change. You want more loyal customers, more sales, bigger margins, more profit, a bigger bonus. What's not to like about change.

But, what are you going to change?

You see, too many of us want change but we are unwilling to change ourselves. As Einstein put it, "Insanity is doing the same thing over and over again and expecting different results."

However, Einstein was wrong. In seeming contradiction, markets continually change. It's inherent in the marketplace. New products, new suppliers, new marketing approaches. And with each the market changes.

As you do the same things over and over again, you will get different results—they'll be worse. Because your competitors will be driving the change.

You will only grow if you change.

Embrace it.

How High Is Up?

When you ask CEOs, "How's business?" you only get two answers. Either the glass is half empty with the bottom in sight or the glass is completely full. Nothing in between. How odd.

A few industries are different: consumer packaged goods sold through retail grocers, air travel, automobiles and trucks. These industries are different because the CEOs know their exact market share. Whether it's from government statistics or independent sources, they know up to the minute where they stand.

For the rest of you, it's half empty or full.

The problem: you don't know how high is up. You think business is great but you might actually be losing market share. Your competitors and the market may be growing much faster than you. But because you're growing and near capacity you think life is rosy. Too bad.

If you don't have the advantage of being in a market with current accurate industry data, you need to develop some sort of measurement. Just because one isn't easily available, doesn't mean you can't develop one on your own.

For example, a company selling building components used strictly in schools used data from construction reporting services. It required some work but they knew where they were.

Why is this important? Suppose you're growing, capacity is great, profits are good. You think all is well with the world. But your competitors are growing faster; the market is growing more rapidly.

Instead of applauding your marketing you should wonder what's wrong.

Instead of your glass being full, it's actually half empty. But you won't know unless you can measure the glass. Your investment and management decisions depend on knowing how well you are doing and you can only know that when you can measure your market.

How high is up?

Have Fun

If you are ever bored, something must be wrong. Marketing means ever-changing. And when you are driving the change, it's fun.

New insights into your customers.

New ideas to help them grow.

New products to try in the market.

All driving your growth.

Growing companies are fun places to work.

New opportunities for advancement.

Profits for more compensation.

More investment in new ideas.

And better morale.

Nothing is quite as much fun as a healthy, growing organization. Anything less is a failure.

Chapter 16

Success

It's been 53 years since Peter Drucker first redefined marketing as the creation and nurturing of customer relationships. Over that time we've experienced these great innovations that have dramatically changed our lives:

Jet travel
Color TV
Cable TV
Microwave ovens
Copiers
Faxes
Voice mail
Cell phones
Desktop computers
The internet

Today CEOs and CMOs turn themselves inside out striving for higher margins, seeking out loyal customers, searching for success in the market. In spite of the remarkable failure rate of 80+%, they continue to introduce new products at an ever-increasing pace.

And, still they carry on, ever faster, to pass by the discipline of marketing.

But a few companies, very profitable, ever-growing, are leading the way.

It is time to follow them; in fact the time to follow passed long ago. It's time to catch up.

Marketing, intelligent, disciplined, aggressive marketing can transform your company.

You can dramatically increase margins and profitability. You can generate successful new products, turning your company into a new product machine, you can have an ever-increasing portfolio of loyal customers.

You can actually feel you have control, not just influence, but control of your top line.

Look at the companies that have done this.

They love their products but they love their customers more.

And that love, that desire to create, build and nurture customer relationships has transformed their businesses, their companies, and their markets.

Once you and your company understand this, internalize this, make it part of your culture, marketing becomes much easier, much less ambiguous.

You develop an intimate understanding of your customers.

The Failure of Marketing

Marketing strategies boil down to a few short but critical sentences.

The 4Ps fall into line as those many tactical decisions become easier, sometimes obvious.

And the management of other marketing activities boils down to a straightforward question:

> What will build our relationship with this customer?

Your business becomes much more fun. And who knows, you might end up with you picture on the cover of *Forbes*.